T0114915

All I have is YOU

life with others!

Cannio Cardozo

WestBow
PRESS®
A DIVISION OF THOMAS NELSON
& ZONDERVAN

WestBow Press books may be ordered through booksellers or by contacting:

WestBow Press
A Division of Thomas Nelson & Zondervan
1663 Liberty Drive
Bloomington, IN 47403
www.westbowpress.com
844-714-3454

Created By
Conrad Gregory, 8/21/2023, 2:14 PM

ISBN: 979-8-3850-1736-2 (sc)
ISBN: 979-8-3850-1737-9 (e)

Library of Congress Control Number: 2024901420

Print information available on the last page.

WestBow Press rev. date: 02/06/2024

Acknowledgment

I express my heartfelt gratitude to God Almighty for the inspiration, guidance and blessings he has bestowed throughout my writing journey. I seize this moment to extend my sincere thanks to Rev. Fr. Silvestre D'Souza (Provincial Superior of Karnataka-Goa Province) for his generosity in granting the permissions and for graciously contributing the foreword to this book.

My appreciation extends to Fr. Lawrence Dmello, Fr. Stephen Pereira, and Fr. Rathan Almeida for generously offering their time and valuable suggestions. I am thankful to Fr. Alexander Braganza, Fr. Jerald D'Souza and Fr. Steny Mascarenhas for their constant encouragement.

I extend my heartfelt appreciation to Fr. Nithesh Rodrigues, Isabel Altamirano, Theresa Kennedy and my family and friends, for their support and prayers.

Last but not least, I would like to thank WestBow Press for their invaluable assistance in making this book a reality.

Foreword

Interpersonal relationships and interdependence cannot be alienated from our life as human beings. This essential aspect of human life has been explored, analysed, and reflected upon from various angles over the centuries by eminent people from different walks of life. "No man is an island", are the immortal words pronounced by the John Donne, the famous English poet and clergyman, who was Dean of St Paul's Cathedral. Martin Buber was an existential philosopher who was known for his philosophy of dialogue centred on the distinction between "I-Thou" and "I-It" relationship.

In the year 2021 Fr Cannio Cardozo brought out his first literary product, "*All I have is I.*" It created ripples within the circle of its readers and enthused him to venture on a sequel, which is now in your hands: "*All I have is You.*" This work shows the originality of the author whose budding talent makes excellent use of what he has read, of what he has studied, and what he has experienced during his years of philosophy and theology, and the early years of his priestly ministry. As I glanced through the book, I could notice elements of psychology, sociology, philosophy and even mysticism. There is a *You* that cannot die. Another notable feature is the daintily crafted poems which summarize each chapter, so we carry with us the essence of what we have read.

I have known Fr Cannio since he was a Seminarian. He is a person who is people-friendly, who can easily mingle with anybody and put them at ease. However, I never imagined he would sit at the table and work with the pen! I am happy to say this is a thought-provoking work that invites reflection as well as discussion. It is my hope that he further nurtures this talent and keeps on surprising us with more and more useful resources which can make our daily living more meaningful and productive.

Hearty congratulations to you, dear Fr Cannio Cardozo.

Fr Silvestre D'Souza OCD
Provincial Superior
Karnataka-Goa Province
Order of Discalced Carmelites

Introduction

Human existence is a situation where we are all linked to one another. We belong to the larger family—society—and society expects us to live at peace with others. United we stand, and divided we fall. Hate divides us, and interdependence unites us, leading to peace. None of us is a pond of stagnant water. If we were, we would dry up, all life within us dying. Only the next rain shower would bring life back again. We need to be like running river water, which mingles with other bodies of water and promotes life. We appear to be independent in our way of life with all our individualism, but we depend a great deal on others for our basic needs. Sharing is the hallmark of interdependence. Saint Francis of Assisi states, "For in giving, we receive." If there is no sharing of talents and resources, then interdependence loses its meaning.

All I Have Is You is about *you* and *me*. *My* roots are in *you*. If *I* am not rooted in *you*, then *I* stand as a dried stick. *You* play a vital role in my life. From the womb till the tomb, *I* require your assistance. We all rely on each other for our various needs. The other important *You* in my life is Almighty God.

All I Have Is You is divided into two parts. In part one, the negative side of "all I have is you" is depicted. Here the focus is on comparing *I* to *you*, with *I* considering that *I* am nothing and desiring *you* and *your* qualities in me. Here you'll notice how *I* get envious of *your* physical features, talents, and possessions and of the people in *your* life.

The second part of the book highlights the importance of *you* in *I*'s life. Its focus is on the positive aspect of *you* in *I*'s life. *You* molds and holds *I* when *I* passes through the storms of life. Every chapter is garnished at the end with a poem summarizing the themes of the chapter.

PART I

Introduction

President Theodore Roosevelt once said, "Comparison is the thief of joy." On comparing ourselves to others, we invite unnecessary sadness into our lives. When we compare ourselves to others and find ourselves wanting, most of the time we are left with a feeling of inferiority. This kind of approach to life creates emotional turbulence within us. Wisdom lies in not comparing ourselves to others.

The poem "Desiderata" (Latin: Things Desired) by Max Ehrmann, written in 1927, became popular in the 1970s. Here is a particularly inspiring stanza: "If you compare yourself with others, you may become vain or bitter, for always there will be greater and lesser persons than yourself. Enjoy your achievements as well as your plans." What matters is looking in the mirror and praising yourself, then taking a peek into the lives of others. I think of Saint Jerome's words when speaking on personal growth: "Good, better, best. Never let it rest till your good is better and your better is best."

In part one, we will go through how a person compares himself or herself with others. In the larger framework of *All I Have Is You*, this first part explores the wish that many have to possess what other people have, such as attractive physical appearance, talents, abilities, family, and position. In wishing these things, a person doesn't think of his or her own worth but is curious about others and their achievements. This causes the *myness* to escape from the self and the *yourness* to be welcomed in, the thought being, *In everything, I wish to be like you.* It would be better to heed the words of George Eliot: "It is never too late to be who you might have been."

Chapter 1

~

I Wish to See Your Qualities in Me

Why do I wish to be made up like you? Why do I always wish to stand on my toes when I'm next to you? Why do I wish to look through eyes that are the same color as yours? Why do I wish to have silky-soft hair just like yours? Why do I wish to have your figure? Why do I wish to have all that is yours, but for myself?

Have you ever wondered why you ask the foregoing questions about your own life? It is all because you place yourself on the weighing scale opposite others. In the effort to look attractive on the outside, you lose your inner peace in the process. It's simple to say, "I wish to see your qualities in me."

The idea is that we want to be in our own spirits but in someone else's body. However, it's essential to consider that true beauty and happiness come from within. Rather than focusing on comparing ourselves with others or trying to replicate others' physical attributes, it may be more beneficial for us to explore and appreciate our own unique virtues, strengths, and aptitudes.

At some point in our lives, we all have felt dissatisfied with our external appearance. The outcome of such negative feelings should not be "I wish to see your qualities in me"; instead, we should embrace those moments as eye-openers. We ought to thank God for blessing us with what others do not have, though we may not be flawless. Our shape, color, and size should not matter when all our body parts are functioning. Comparing ourselves to others or yearning to look like someone else is often a fruitless venture that leads only to further discontentment. Recognizing that there are individuals who face challenges in terms of physical ability can help us realize what we have and cultivate a greater sense of gratitude toward God.

It's essential to embrace self-acceptance and recognize that beauty comes in diverse forms. Our internal form should not determine our worth or our happiness. True beauty comes from accepting ourselves as we are and nurturing a positive self-image based on our inner selves.

When we mull over nature, it teaches us that there is beauty in diversity. The mountains in the countryside display the splendor of nature. When we see them from afar, they seem to be enormous, irregular, and staggering. If we take a closer look at them, we will find that they follow no ordered plan. Every plant and tree adds beauty to the mountain range. Short or tall, fat or slim, each plays its role accordingly. Similarly, we come in different sizes, shapes, and colors, and our diversity embellishes our society.

We are human beings first and individual bodies second. As the uniqueness of all flora collectively forms the diverse landscapes, we too, as individuals of different races, embellish humanity. Even the animals we perceive have their own identities in terms of form, shape, and size. No other creature except the human being feels ashamed of its looks. This may be because we are rational beings. Actually, our thinking faculties should help us accept ourselves as we are. However, sometimes we feel small in front of others. Dr. Lindsay Kite, coauthor of the book *More Than a Body: Your Body Is an Instrument, Not an Ornament*, writes, "Loving your body isn't thinking your body looks good. It is knowing your body is good regardless of how it looks."

To obtain a better understanding, let us look at the example of Robin, Jack's friend. Jack and Robin had joined the same hostel and were together twenty-four-seven. Robin always stood with his face down or with it hidden behind others' heads in group photographs. Every month, he changed his hairstyle to imitate others, yet he was not content with his face.

One night, when the dormitory was silent and dark, Jack was in the corner bed. Some of the students had pushed their beds closer to the pedestal fans, and others were sleeping half naked. It was the dog days of summer. When all were sleeping like logs, Robin's blanket was covering his whole body, his sweat causing it to stick to his skin. In addition to that, the top portion of the blanket was moving up and down. This aroused Jack's curiosity. He shook the shoulder of his friend who was sleeping in the next bed to wake him. Both of them tiptoed over to Robin. After approaching Robin's bed, Jack pinched Robin and pulled out the blanket. His friend nearly jumped out of his skin. Before Jack could shout and wake any of the others, his friend covered his mouth with his hand. Robin, whose face had gone white, tuned toward Jack and punched him in the stomach. Before Robin could get out of his bed and on his feet, Jack and his friend ran to the toilet section. There they had a barrel of laughs because Robin's face looked as if it had been dipped in a bucket of fairness cream. On that day, they rejoiced, but Robin was in tears. He always felt that because he was dark in complexion, no one liked him. He shed his tears and spent his energy comparing himself to others instead of accepting himself as he was. That always hindered him from improving his personality.

Beneath the Shallows

Our physical bodies are the receptors of all five types of sensory input. The philosophical school of empiricism believes that sensual experiences cannot misguide us and that knowledge is primarily gained from the interaction of the five senses with the external world. The recurring sensory experiences create the concept of the world in our minds. However, there are some other philosophical schools that disagree with empiricism, especially rationalism, which argues that there are fundamental truths or innate concepts that exist independently of sensory input and that these are accessible through intellectual manifestation or intuition.

Both empiricism and rationalism contribute to our understanding of the world, and both perspectives have merits. While empiricism highlights the value of sensory experiences in influencing our knowledge, rationalism emphasizes the role of cognition and innate ideas. A balanced approach that integrates both empirical observations and rational thinking often leads to a more comprehensive understanding of the world. Acknowledging the role of our senses in gathering information, while also considering the power of reason and reflection, can help us navigate life and make sense of its complexities. In our day-to-day lives, it makes sense that our senses provide much of our knowledge.

In this section, "Beneath the Shallows," we are leaning more toward the empirical approach. This means beneath our physical appearance, our senses play a vital role in the molding of our lives. Our physical selves are always sat a shallow level, and our five senses are at a deeper level, from which they run the show by interacting with our current surroundings.

Picture yourself walking barefoot by the seashore, feeling the warm sand beneath your feet, viewing the vast deep blue ocean, hearing the relaxing sound of the rolling waves, smelling the saltiness in the breeze, and tasting the specks of salt that have formed on your lips. In this setting, all your senses are engaged, feeding you a rich and immersive experience.

The five senses along with the brain handle our reactions. There are times when we disregard our senses and pay attention only to our external selves. This is like admiring a new-model BMW but ignoring the chassis that supports it. Let us get a better understating with the following example:

A day of one-eye blindness in my life enlightened me. A week prior to the blindness, I had an infection in my right eye. Initially, I did nothing about it, and there was no sign of improvement. One day, I visited an optician. She gave me eye drops, believing it to be an external infection, and said, "If it gets worse, come and see me tomorrow." She had no doubt that this would be my first and last visit to her. I faithfully followed her orders and used my prescription, but my eye was losing more of its ability to see day by day. Without much delay, on next morning I rushed to the optician. She was bewildered and referred me to an ophthalmologist. Unfortunately, the ophthalmologist was unavailable that day, and the following day was a statutory holiday. The optician assured me that with her influence, she would get an appointment for me with a doctor at a private clinic. While I was leaving her consulting room, she said, "The situation is critical."Her words made my blood run cold.

Those words echoed in my ears, and I had a sleepless night. I opened my eyes in the morning, but one eye was utterly blind. No tea or coffee would comfort me, only the voice of an ophthalmologist. My ears were both open to hear the phone ring. When I received a call from the ophthalmologist, I was momentarily relieved. I rushed to him wearing sunglasses. He examined the condition of my eye. He shook like a leaf, not knowing what was wrong inside my eye, and said, "You have to do these tests before it gets worse. Right now, I can't say anything." At that moment, I was quaking in my boots because even the doctor could not identify the problem.

Since it was a holiday, no labs were open. At the same time, there was a rumor in the air that because of the COVID-19 vaccine, many had lost their sight, but I didn't know how true that was. Nevertheless, at that moment, I was tempted to think that I may be one of those people. Many more negative thoughts occurred in my mind.

I visited almost all the labs in the city, and all of them were closed. The doctor panicked and gave me a letter to give to the emergency department at the hospital. In the evening, after going through the reports, he still wasn't sure about the cause of my sight loss. He told the nurse to put me on steroids. That night, with the steroids, my eyesight was restored. And that morning, I had a peaceful, extended sleep.

I am relating this incident before you to impress upon you that our eyesight is worth a great deal. That night, I prayed to God, saying I would have no regrets if He would reduce the size of my eye, or cause it to squint, or force me to wear spectacles as long as He did not to take my sight away. Having a functioning eye is more important than just having a physical eye. Having a nonfunctioning eye is like having legs yet not being able to walk because of paralysis.

What lies in the deeps is equally important as what is in the shallows. In my case, what was in the deeps was my eyesight, and what was in the shallows was my eye.

It does not matter whether you have small eyes or squint-eyes, or brown eyes or blue eyes: what is crucial is sight.

An Original Copy

Everyone is special. Whether you have a fat nose or a squint-eye, what matters is *you*. You are the only one of your type available. None of us can change many things about the original copy that we are born with. To some extent, our physical can be modified but is hard to replace. We need to be grateful and happy because we are alive and are a part of this beautiful world. Why then complain about the aging body, which will soon be unappealing? It's important to acknowledge and appreciate our inherent worth regardless of external factors such as appearance and age. Our true essence lies within us that is, our values, character, outlook toward life, etc.

Be proud! You are an original copy. No one can take your place in another's life. Young or old, you remain what you are. Only the body's growth and expansion are visible. When we compare ourselves with others, our own sense of self-worth lessens.

Consider this story of a young man: Sickness had prevented him from living freely since his birth. He was tiny and feeble. His fragile body would not allow him to be active in sports. Other boys his age looked hale and healthy. In due course, he joined a religious ministry. Once again, his illness prevented him from catering to the needs of the worshippers.

Though the circumstances forced him to quit, he did not give up on himself. He believed he was the only copy, and indeed he was. In most aspects, he differed from others. He stopped dwelling on his weaknesses.

The young man had a passion for music. He was sad about the church music as it was dull in nature. Somebody persuaded him to write some hymns to convey a message of hope and joy. He took it as a challenge and wrote more than six hundred hymns. In 1748, when he died, he left behind the most valuable compilation of hymns in the world. This young man was none other than Isaac Watts, who gave us the famous carol "Joy to the World." This success was possible in his life because he believed he was special and that there was no one else like him.

Beauty Is Only Skin-Deep

Some think they are perfect when they are not, and others think they are imperfect when they are not. This appears to be a contradictory statement, with wisdom lying in between the two extremes. Those who are proud and overconfident with perfect bodies entertain an illusion of perfection because there is no set standard for human appearance. That is why the Greek philosopher Plato wisely said, "Beauty is in the eye of the beholder." William Shakespeare's version of it is "Beauty is brought by the judgment of the eye," which means that physical beauty is relative. Who is beautiful in your eyes may not be beautiful to me. For example, for a child, her mother may be more beautiful than Miss Universe. For a lover, his woman is more beautiful than Miss World. This means there is no perfect external beauty.

Indeed, common standards of beauty often generate an illusion of perfection, leading some individuals to believe they must conform to a specific ideal. However, in reality, there is no universal standard for perfect external beauty. Every person has his or her own unique features, qualities, and charisma, which are appreciated by different individuals in various ways.

Beauty encompasses a wide range of aspects beyond physical appearance, including kindness, intelligence, and sympathy—inner attributes. True beauty emanates from within a person and is reflected in his or her actions, character, and thoughts. By acknowledging the subjective nature of beauty and focusing on developing our inner qualities, we can cultivate a more inclusive and accepting perspective. Celebrating diversity and recognizing the beauty in ourselves and others, beyond outward looks, can lead to a greater appreciation of the inherent uniqueness and value of every individual.

Those who think that they are imperfect have the wrong impression that others are perfect. Just because I may not look like others does not mean I am imperfect. We all have the same physical parts. What makes us different is the wrapping and the size. Comparing yourself to others is like trying to hide in others' shade and, in doing so, never growing freely as you ought. If you do this, you need to come into light and be healed of your so-called imperfections.

Let us take the example of a coconut tree. If we plant a coconut sapling under the shade of an enormous tree, the sapling will make all every effort to break through and come out into the sunlight. In the process of its search for sunlight, the tree is compelled to bend and twist. It is amid the reality of thick trees all around it and does not feel bad that the other trees are doing well. It accepts its surroundings as a challenge. The outcome of its struggle is seen after a few years. The coconut tree also enjoys the sunlight as other trees do.

Initially, it is hard to admit to our imperfections. When we focus on our goals and dreams, we forget about our external beauty. The coconut tree has to be all twisted to attain the sunlight. We too have to twist and turn while accomplishing our dreams.

We are expected to strike a balance between perfect and imperfect physical appearance. The so-called perfect person will lose all his or her beauty as age swallows it. That can cause irrational anxiety. Thinking that he or she had always had an imperfect physique can hinder the person in achieving things in life.

Here is an incident as told by a mother: Lilly received a phone call from Viola to invite her to her birthday party. "But please dress simple," Viola said. Lilly changed her outfit five times just to get confirmation from her mother that the frock she had on was indeed simple. A pretty face cannot lie. It reveals the truth apart from any clothing. Lilly stepped into Viola's house. Viola could not hold back her emotions. She said, "Oh, Lilly, you look so appealing. Now I have to change my dress. I told you to wear something simple." They walked into a posh room, and in the closet were many expensive dresses. Lilly said in her mind, *Viola looks great in that dress, but even if she were to wear all the dresses, unless she sets her thinking right, she will always feel she does not look good.* Viola tried six outfits. The seventh one, she wore for her birthday party at a popular restaurant. The frock was remarkable, but envy had stolen Viola's smile, so her expression remained dismal.

There is an illusion among young people today that the best things make us beautiful. In reality, the way we project ourselves, namely, with confidence, is what makes us truly attractive. Beauty is skin-deep: how much can you impress others with expensive things? And at last, your beauty will fade. Confidence is indeed a significant factor that can enhance your magnetism. When you project self-assurance and embrace your unique qualities, it positively impacts the way others perceive you. People are often drawn to individuals who radiate confidence and authenticity.

While material possessions or external appearance may initially capture people's attention, these things do not define true beauty in the long run. Material things are transient and do not accompany us throughout our lives. What truly matters is how we connect with others, that we make a positive impact, and that we cultivate our inner qualities.

Actuality to Potentiality

Aristotle was a well-known figure in ancient Greek philosophy. His significant contributions were in the fields of logic, metaphysics mathematics, politics, ethics, and other sciences. When he was dealing with form and matter in detail, he introduced the two terms *potentially* and *actuality*.

Potentiality and *potency* are translations of the Greek word *dunamis*, which does not speak of the mode in which an object exists. It refers to the power, ability, or faculty of a thing to make a changeover to different states. *Actuality* is a translation of a Greek word *energeia* In contrast to potentiality, actuality is the motion, the change, or the final product of possibility. Let me explain these terms in simple words with an example that Aristotle himself formed. Potentiality is the possibility of performing something or becoming something, and actuality is the achievement of the potential. Aristotle's famous example is of an acorn, which precedes the oak that it grows into. For him, the acorn is the potential state of an oak tree. The oak tree is the changed version of the acorn, and that Aristotle calls the actuality.

My purpose in explaining these concepts of Aristotle is to apply them so we may comprehend the physical reality of human beings. I would like to reverse the order here, with *actuality* first and *potentiality* second. Every seed is the actual state, but it has the potential to become a tree.

In our lives, what matters is what we are right now, right here, which is our actual state. At this stage of life, I may be a child, an adult, or an old person. This illustrates my actual state in time. The potential within me is what I can become: a doctor, teacher, painter, chauffeur, lawyer, and so on. This may apply to a child or an adult. And those of us who are older adults may think, *What about us? What can we become?* We can become good listeners, gardeners, father figures, writers, advisers, intercessors, and so forth. I believe no one is hopeless. Everyone is unique and useful in his or her own way. Therefore, the potential to become something does not end.

One major mistake that we make is to fix our attention only on our actuality. For example, we complain: "Oh, I am short. Will they accept me on the sports team?" We might say, "I am not good-looking," or "I am dark in complexion," or "I am old." We might ask, "What great thing can I do?" We are stuck on our outer appearance and cannot focus on what we can become. We cover our potentialities with our appearance. As a result, we always wish to see other people's characteristics in ourselves. By solely concentrating on our exterior appearance, we may hinder our personal growth and limit ourselves from discovering our true potential. It's essential to shift our perspective and recognize that our worth and potential extend far beyond our physical appearance.

Each of us inherits a set of abilities and potentialities that are independent of our outward appearance. By nurturing and developing these qualities, we can unlock our true potential and make significant contributions to the world.

Social Expectations

An intellectual by the name of Friedrich Schiller, an eighteenth-century dramatist, once said, "Appearance rules the world." And this is all because of what society demands. There is constant pressure on a girl to be slim and trim. If she is not, then she will not be liked by guys. We expect woman to have an ideal appearance, like that of a Barbie doll. Men are expected to have a V-shape body and are always welcomed when they are tall. Individuals are compelled to have perfect bodies according to others' opinions. The existing framework of our society plays a significant role in narrowing our attention down to focus only on physical appearance.

It is unfortunate that these societal stresses can lead individuals to develop a negative body image, low self-esteem, and feelings of inadequacy. The pressure to have an ideal appearance, such as being slim, having a certain body shape, or possessing certain physical features, can be overwhelming and detrimental to our well-being. These standards are reinforced by the media, advertisements, and cultural customs, which can perpetuate narrow definitions of beauty.

Social media, especially Facebook and Instagram, make an enormous impact on young minds and perpetuate the crisis of obsession over external appearance. It eventually ends up with an individual's having an untrue idea of perfection, such as unblemished skin. A little bit of acne on a pretty face is enough for a person's self-image to plummet. A college friend of mine once said, "Every time a new pimple pops out on my face, I feel blue and become aware of what others will think of me. I have no options. If I squeeze the pimple, it swells, and if I cover it with makeup, everyone looks at me as if I they don't know me. I just leave the pimple uncovered for everyone to notice it, hoping that it will go away in time. And when it does, another pops up." When we experience a hormonal change in our bodies, we should always remember that this is temporary. It will not occur in the future. A pimple can influence and interfere with our mood, causing a person to behave differently for an entire day. We are too much into the ideal of beauty, which does not matter in the broader scope of life. We should endeavor to divert focus our attention on our goals and encourage our friends to do the same. In the end, physical appearance is only one part of the personality.

Perceive yourself in yourself and not in others.

It is only at some stages of our lives that we feel we should look better than others. Prior to our teenage years, we are not much bothered about our external beauty. By the late sixties, many people are less bothered about their external appearance. After all, when we reach old age, everything vanishes. "But the Lord said to Samuel, 'Do not consider his appearance or his height, for I have rejected him.' The Lord does not look at the things people look at. People look at the outward appearance, but the Lord looks at the heart" (1 Samuel 16:7) For God, who is unchangeable, every changeable being is a passing reality. So what matters is the soul, not the body.

It is crucial to pay attention to how we react after seeing our external selves in the mirror. The aftermath of this will build our confidence. Here is an inspiring anonymous quote: "Be a witness, not a judge. Focus on yourself, not on others. Listen to your heart, not to the crowd." Listen to your heart; it has all the answers to your problems.

Out of Our Control

Our birth is not within our control. We might have been born on any continent in the world. What is essential is how we transform ourselves after our births. We are helpless in remolding or redesigning our physical bodies. Our ability to grow, learn, and transform is not limited by our physical bodies. We can strive to become better versions of ourselves by developing qualities such as empathy, kindness, and wisdom. We can pursue education, acquire new skills, cultivate significant relationships, and contribute positively to the world.

Following is an example of accepting what is not within our control: Tina was born in an aristocratic family and enjoyed the best things in life. Every day, she would ride in an air-conditioned car. On one occasion, she entered her examination hall carrying a writing pad and a textbook. The classroom was in total silence. Everyone's eyes were on their books, studying up until the last moment. With a load of exam papers, the invigilator entered and requested that everyone place all their books outside the classroom. While closing her book, Tina realized she had forgotten her pencil case in her car. This was because she had feared the examination. Her blood ran cold, and sweat formed on her face. Cracking her knuckles, she entered the room, leaving her textbook outside.

On reaching her desk, she turned back. A girl with unshaped eyebrows, unpolished nails, and an unironed shirt looked her in the eye. Tina said, "Please, can I borrow a pen from you?"

"Yes! Definitely," the girl said, handing her a heavy antique pen with a broad nib. Tina stared at it with a sad face and imagined her fine pens, all of them contemporary. She took the pen and wrote her name and roll number on the answer paper. She felt the pen's heft. It was without a buckle.

As she held the question paper in her hands, a thought popped into her mind: *If I continue to complain about the pen, I will not finish writing the answers to these easy questions and will not pass the exam with flying colors.*

Many of us complain about the external appearance of our bodies and miss the train of life. We fail to accept that we are each the only copy of ourselves. In the foregoing example, the pen is our body. Many of us may think we may not have an ideal physical appearance. Tina didn't think that the pen she had borrowed was very attractive. But when she took her attention off the external qualities of the pen and focused on what the pen could do, she found that it could do the same thing that all other pens could do, that is, write. And in this example, the question paper is life. Tina's attention was on what she could do with a pen and not on what she could not change about it. She believed that the externals of the pen did not matter. What mattered was what she wrote on the lines of the paper. This led her to score well on the exam. It all happened because she was aware of what she was engrossed in and not what she was doing.

Fall in Love with Your Body

Someone said rightly, "Fall in love with taking care of yourself, mind, body, and spirit." We must take care of our bodies. Grooming ourselves and presenting ourselves well can boost our confidence and contribute to a positive self-image. It is natural for individuals to want to look and feel their best. No one likes to be barbarian or uncouth. The top secrets to a healthy body are regular physical exercise and nutritious food. Fragrances and cosmetics are to be used in presenting ourselves to the public, not for making an impression. All these things in moderation are excellent, but in excess they are harmful.

Excessive focus on external appearance or obsession with physical perfection can lead to unhealthy behavior or negative self-perception. It is crucial to know that true beauty and self-worth go beyond external appearances. For example, a young woman may look gorgeous in a sari, but this does not mean that she wears a sari on all occasions, even when going mountain climbing. We need to know what will look good on our bodies and what to wear and where. When we present ourselves moderately, it means we have accepted our bodies and are working on maintenance and disease prevention. I know a man who wanted to reduce his stubborn belly fat. He was not interested in comparing himself with others. His intention was pure: to get fit. This is not a case of wanting to see others' qualities in himself; it is one of seeing himself in himself.

The most important thing is to feel comfortable and confident in your own skin. Dressing well should be an expression of your genuine self and not something based on the opinions of others.

LOOKS

Whether you are short or tall,
Tell the world that you don't care at all.
Whether you are slim or fat,
Tell the world that your goal is set.
Whether you are bald or hairy,
Tell the world that only the purposeless worry.
Whether you are dark or fair,
Tell the world that only those who are preoccupied care.
Whether your eyes are dark or light,
Tell the world the only a thief's eyes lie.
Whether you have pimples or wrinkles,
Tell the world of your endless goals.
Whether you have a beauty mark or a dimple,
Tell the world of your life that is simple.

Chapter 2

~

I Wish Your Qualities Were Mine

The chapter title "I Wish Your Qualities Were Mine" refers to the talents and abilities that other people possess. I remain silent and am sad upon seeing you excel in life. You shine like a star, and I am trampled underfoot like dirt. No one wishes to be my friend, but everyone appreciates you and wants to snap a photograph with you. If I was given a chance to choose which the talents, I would choose all the ones that you have. Why does no one applaud when I sing or dance? When I am standing next to you, why do others call you forward to speak and not me? Why can't I do that you can? Why am I not special like you? These and many more thoughts sometimes pop into our minds. Whether subconsciously or consciously, we desire to have others' talents for ourselves. These talents, the things that we are best at, play a vital role in our growth.

Rather than pondering on what we lack, we should embrace our own abilities and invest our energy into improving them. Each one of us has something to offer, and humankind needs varied, talented people. In nurturing our capacities, we at least have something offer to our communities and develop a positive impression of our distinctive way of life. Each one of us in our respective journeys has prospects for improvement and fulfillment. It gets us nowhere if we long for others' talents. We need to embrace ourselves, explore our passions, and nurture our exclusive talents. True fulfillment and happiness come from accepting and celebrating what we are rather than envying others.

We all are special, and that is why we cannot be like others. If we were all the same, then we would not be special. All of us on this earth are like packets with different contents. The rating of some of the content is higher for some and less for others. The fact remains that everyone is filled with at least something. Since everyone is given something, we are expected to excel with what we are given. There is an inspiring quote that goes, "A child is like a butterfly in the wind. Some can fly higher than others, but each one flies the best it can. Why compare one against the other? Each one is special; each one is beautiful."

Let us better understand this concept by using imagery from a flower garden. At dawn one day, the flowers in the garden were interacting. Gladiolus said to Jasmine, "I want to have your scent, which attracts Hindu women. They adorn their hair with you on important occasions."

Jasmine replied, "I want the strength that you have. You remain long after being detached from your stem. I, on the other hand, get weak, drooping within a day."

Gladiolus said, "Even with having that special trait, I am not found near the deities. In your case, your garlands adorn the deities. You get the chance to be close to the heart of the gods and goddesses."

The aloe vera plant, having overheard everything, said, "Please do not wish to be each other. Be happy about what you are. Look at me. I produce neither flowers nor scent. I am used in cosmetics, and for that I have to give myself completely. Yet I am not recognized as you are. The companies steal my thunder, and at my cost, they become prosperous."

The only sound around was the buzzing of the bees, which passed a message of self-acceptance to all other flowers.

Everyone has something to offer. Jasmine has a delightful fragrance. The gladiolus is blessed with durability. The quality of aloe vera goes unnoticed, unlike others, but it is equally important, like others. Every individual has something to offer, whether small or big.

Talent Stealing

There are times when people are so frustrated that they feel like stealing someone else's talents in order to become popular. The tiger can be tamed, but there is no guarantee that it will always behave well. Though we may tame ourselves by stealing others' talents, we cannot always change our innate talents according to our own preferences. My yearning to have your qualities for myself is stronger when I spend sleepless nights contemplating others' talents.

We are appreciated when we focus, not on others, but on ourselves. Everyone has areas where they excel and struggle. This is perfectly OK. It does not mean that to avoid struggle, we should desire to steal the talents of others. Though it is not possible to steal others' talents, knowing that they have them keeps us unhappy. What we must do is channel our own energy instead of comparing ourselves to others. We need to learn to identify our own passions and talents and our commitment to build on those God-given gifts. Success enters our lives when we embrace our passions and kick out our desire to imitate others.

Everyone is born with the ability to be someone. Yes! Talents are innate. Some are born with talents such as acting, singing, and athletics, all of which are popular. And those who excel in them easily go on to become celebrities. There are many other talents that most of the time go unnoticed, such as cooking, gardening, and listening.

The fact is, none of us can steal another person's talents. Everyone has something to offer to society. When I am given a gift to share with others, why should I envy the gifts that others have? Feeling sorry for myself for not having the finest talents does not explain my unhappiness.

Sometimes we spend a great deal of time pondering on others' gifts and neglecting what we ourselves have. "Talent is a universal gift, but it takes a lot of courage to use it. Don't be afraid to be the best," writes Paulo Coelho. We should not be afraid to work on our talents and be outstanding with what we have.

Here I want to introduce you to two facts: ideal facts and actual facts. Ideal facts are facts that an individual always thinks of, things that he or she wishes to be. These are best explained as an individual's dreams. These ideal facts sometimes remain only in the mind. Actual facts are the facts of putting in the effort to be someone, being industrious to achieve set goals.

The best example that comes to my mind is my daddy. He was once told by someone when learning to play violin, "Practice makes perfect." My dad ultimately found this to be true in his own life. His ideal fact was to be like his father, a musician by profession. He played trumpet at church. My father did not linger in those ideal facts; he worked on them. He did not remain idle in terms of achieving his ideal facts. In actual fact, he worked hard to become a musician. He mastered the violin at a young age. Other than playing at church functions, he did nothing else with it. He put his heart and soul into learning the clarinet to get into the Indian Navy Band. Though an only son, he had the responsibility of cultivating his father's land, but he never gave up on pursuing his dreams.

Many of us die with only our ideal facts. This is made evident when we hear people saying, "I have an excellent story to tell and want to write a book." If they do not ever pick up a pen to write, then they will only write a book when pigs fly. Their ideal fact is to write a book, but they put no effort toward achieving this goal in their day-to-day lives. Such people only wish that they had the talents of someone else, doing nothing to cultivate their own talents. It is good to dream sometimes, but one must see to it that some of these dreams are actualized.

Let's look at the parable of the talents from the Holy Bible. In the parable, a master goes on a journey to a distant land. Prior to that, he summons three of his servants and hands over to them talents according to their abilities. To the last servant, he gave one talent; to the second, he gave two; and to the first, he entrusted five talents. In the master's absence, the first and the second servants made the utmost use of the talents they had been given. They multiplied what they had. It didn't happen overnight; they kept their noses to the grindstone. The last servant wanted to avoid his master's wrath so he failed to make any profit by burying the talent in the ground.

When the master returned, he requested an accounting. The first servant came forth with five additional talents; the second, with two additional; and the last one with only the one he had been given. The master rewarded the first two servants, and he took the one talent away from the last one. If you and I make no use of our God-given talents, then they will be snatched away from us. We can compare this to a machine that is not in use. If unused for a long time, it develops rust and becomes useless.

These words of Robin Sharma speak to this parable: "Why hide your talent in the closet of complacency when you have greatness within you?" God gives us talents so we may make the best use of them. Talents are not showpieces. The more you put your talents to use, the better you become as a person. Developing a talent raises your self-confidence. "If you have talent, use it in every way possible. Don't hoard it. Don't dole it out like a miser. Squander it, like a millionaire, intent on going broke," says Brenda Francis.

Stephen King says, "Talent is never static. It's always growing or dying." If an individual is not growing his or her given talents, then those innate talents become obsolete. The following example will shed light on this:

"I was tortured by my parents to learn violin since my cousins were experts at playing it." These are the words of a professional soccer player. His mom was fond of music. She had a desire to learn a musical instrument. Unfortunately, her conditions at home were unsupportive of a venture into music as her livelihood. Her brother's children had picked up the skill of playing the violin at a very early age, so she pushed her son to hold a violin. Whenever she told her son to follow the example of his cousins, it would drive him up the wall. She hoped to see her dream realized in her son. Her obsession forced her to think that her son could do it. For almost a year it was his obligation to play the violin every day. If he didn't do that, then she would not serve him any food. Finally, she realized that violin was not his cup of tea, as his heart was on soccer.

Years later, this woman's son became a famous soccer player. At that point he asked his mom, "Do my cousins still play the violin?" She had no words because his cousins, other than when they were learning to play, never again touched a violin. Today they have lost the touch to play the violin well. They are busy running their family business.

Range of Intelligence

Everybody is a whiz kid. We can't judge a water creature by its ability to climb a mountain. If we do this, the creature will live its entire life believing that it is incompatible with society. Yes, everybody is a genius in one way or another. We must give consistent support and care to everyone who is not excelling in finding their talents.

Howard Gardner, a psychologist and a professor at Harvard University, is the pioneer of the theory of multiple intelligences, which is the subject of his book *Frames of Mind*, published in 1983. In *Frames of Mind*, Gardner lays down eight types of human intelligence. Let's take a look at these:

1. Visual/spatial intelligence
    Individuals in this category possess a gift to think abstractly and multi- dimensionally. Using their imaginations and being creative is their cup of tea.

2. Bodily/kinesthetic intelligence
   These individuals have the gift of great physical ability. They have amazing hand-eye coordination. To put it simply, they are good at physical activities such as sports.

3. Musical intelligence
   Individuals with this type of intelligence are blessed with an ear for music and are good at such things as pitch, meter, rhythm, tone, and melody. Their ability to learn music and play musical instruments is phenomenal.

4. Linguistic/verbal intelligence
   The individuals who possess this type of intelligence have the innate talents of writing and speaking. They are good at choosing words and at sounds. They have the ability to communicate their thoughts in black and white.

5. Logical/mathematical intelligence
   People with this type of intelligence have the capability to break down problems logically. These individuals are good at numbers, reasoning, and analyzing.

6. Interpersonal intelligence
   People with this gift are able to understand others' moods, feelings, temperaments, and motivations. They can easily grab others' attention and are able to make friends easily.

7. Intrapersonal intelligence
   People with intrapersonal intelligence can effortlessly become aware of their own feelings, emotional states, and goals. They enjoy introspection, surveying their relationships with others, and measuring their own positives points.

8. Naturalistic intelligence
    This eighth type of intelligence was not a part of Gardner's original writings. He proposed it in 1995. These words of his make it clear: "If I were to rewrite *Frames of Mind* today, I would probably add an eighth intelligence: the intelligence of the naturalist. It seems to me that the individual who is readily able to recognize flora and fauna, to make other consequential distinctions in the natural world, and to use this ability productively (in hunting, in farming, in biological science) is exercising an important intelligence and one that is not adequately encompassed in the current list." In simple words, naturalistic intelligence involves the ability to grasp the signs of nature.

An individual can possess more than one type of intelligence in her or his lifetime.

When we assess ourselves, we need to consider asking the opinion of the person with whom we are closest. Acquiring a deep understanding of our abilities gives us a clearer view of how to reach our goals in our personal life and our professional life.

If we wish to learn to be excellent at something, we must first understand the types of intelligence we possess, then gear up and build upon our strengths. There is an inspiring saying, "Don't compare your child with others. There's no comparison between the sun and the moon. They each shine when it's their time." We all have different types of intelligence, so it is futile to compare ourselves with others.

Indeed, the diverse nature of intelligence makes it futile to make direct comparisons among individuals. Every individual inherits his or her own distinct combination of intelligence types. This enhances the person's unique personality.

Environmental Factors

Environmental factors play a significant role in the development of an individual's talents. For instance, when an individual is born and raised in a poor environment, even if the person is blessed with talents, he or she may not have the chance to improve on them. It is like having an enormous field but no oxen to till the ground. The field represents the inherited abilities an individual possesses. The ox stands for the facilities and resources that facilitates the person's cultivating and polishing his or her talents. Without these essential resources and opportunities, even the most gifted people have a tough time fully developing and showcasing their talents.

Improper socioeconomic situations and other various environmental factors limit the support, resources, and opportunities that we require to discover and develop our talents. Fewer opportunities to be educated in a particular field and total lack of opportunities can indeed hamper the realization of our potential.

Let me share with you the story of an underprivileged woman. In August 2019, a video of a woman singing at Ranaghat railway station in West Bengal went viral. Ranu Mondal was her name, and she achieved fame overnight. She was a gifted singer and had been born in utter poverty. She had four children, but none of them took care of her after her husband's death. An engineer hailing from Ranaghat in West Bengal noticed her singing some Bollywood hits and uploaded a video of her doing so on his Facebook page.

This woman with a torn sari, buckteeth, and unkempt hair singing those songs left a lasting impression on the people who viewed the video. The video caught the attention of a renowned Bollywood singer, who called Ranu Mondal to record a music video. That too went viral.

This is the best example of poor living conditions hampering one's ability to succeed at using one's talents. If Ranu had been born into a rich or famous family, she would have had ample opportunities to refine her talent.

Many people lack opportunities to work on their talents. But there are some who don't think poverty is the reason why people fail to excel at their talents. Individuals who are positive about their abilities may have numerous reasons to feel bad about the environments in which they live; still they find a reason to be happy in doing what they like.

In any situation, we should not let go of our talents. Bill Gates says, "If you are born poor, it is not your mistake, but if you die poor, it is your mistake." This statement calls everyone to be industrious, although this statement isn't generalized, including people who live in developing countries and do not have the basic necessities to live.

Self-Realization to Self-Actualization

Self-realization is the starting point of inner happiness. When a person identifies his or her strengths, it shows in his or her level of contentment. Self-realization does not happen overnight. It involves a constant process of learning from failures and discouragements. When an individual understands and accepts who he or she is, he or she is filled with inner peace and bliss that is not dependent on external circumstances. George Bernard Shaw puts it in this beautiful way: "Life isn't about finding yourself. Life is about creating yourself." We all need to create our own identity, and for that, we have to believe in ourselves.

However, self-realization involves accepting oneself and embracing one's distinctiveness. It is about being genuine and true to oneself, and not about seeking approval from external sources. Self-realization is a private, personal journey. It demands introspection, commitment, and self-compassion if the self-realization is to be successful. Through this process, an individual discovers his or her real potential and finds great satisfaction in life, living meaningfully.

There is no fun in lying low after self-realization. We have to work on what is revealed to us about ourselves. Bruce Lee would say, "Absorb what is useful; discard what is not; add what is uniquely your own." To attain self-actualization, we have to discard what is not ours. We must let go of the talents that we are not blessed with and focus on what we have. We must ignore what we cannot achieve and build up what we have got.

If self-realization is exploration of oneself, then self-actualization is polishing that which one has discovered while exploring. A parable of an old beggar and his son will help us understand this idea. Many moons ago, there lived an aged beggar. He begged throughout his lifetime and took care of his son. Rain or shine, he would sit on the ground crossed-leg on a city street. When he was on his deathbed, he called his son and said, "Son! I have nothing to give you except this begging bowl." Placing his hand into his son's, he kicked the bucket.

His son was helpless and felt compelled to walk in his father's footsteps. He was also wise as an owl. He thought outside the box and changed the spot to beg, moving from the city street to a place outside a theater and near a park. It turned out to be impressive move, yet he did not make enough money. Then he had the thought of acting blind to attract more people. He placed a placard saying, "You are my eyes! Please don't ignore me." This worked a bit, but not according to his expectations.

After racking his brains for a long time, he considered a paradigm shift. His father had always told him that if he disguised himself as someone miserable, he would gain people's sympathy and they would drop a penny in his bowl. He did exactly the opposite of what his father had said. He clipped his hair and put on clothes that were neat. This attempt turned out to be his greatest failure, though.

After that, he went through some sleepless nights. One night, he dreamt of his father and of God. With the thought of God lingering in his mind, an idea came to him. The next day, he took a stunning statue of Lord Shiva with him to the begging spot. The begging bowl that his father had given him did not match the beauty of the statue, so he cleaned it. As the dirt was wiped away, the bowl started shining. At last it was revealed to be a golden bowl.

The son was restless and tried every way he could think of to be the best. Though all his efforts failed, he did not give up. Once he realized that the bowl was gold, he discontinued begging.

Self-realization comes all of a sudden, but with a great deal of effort. To reach the level of self-realization is like finding gold within oneself. As in the parable, the son discovered gold in the thing that he already had. Swami Sivananda says, "The harder the struggle, the more glorious the triumph. Initially, it is a struggle to discover oneself."

An important thing to keep in mind is that after discovering the gold, the son could not remain idle. He had to invest his money to have better prospects in life. This is self-actualization. Similarly, after eliminating all the lesser choices and coming to the best one, we cannot sit quietly by if we wish to pass from self-realization to self-actualization.

Fear the Lie of Failure

Success and failure are part and parcel of everyone's life. We fear failure most of the time. Actually, every failure is rung on the ladder of success. Many successful people have met with many hindrances and undergone many failures before finally achieving their goals, which is possible to do with perseverance, determination, and openness to learning from past failures, which ultimately leads to success. Paulo Coelho writes about achieving one's dreams: "There is only one thing that makes a dream impossible to achieve: the fear of failure."

Failure sometimes pushes us toward valuable insights, lessons, and chances that can change our lives. It enables us to collect ourselves after feeling broken to develop resilience and refine our outlook. We have to see each failure as a learning experience, giving us feedback about what doesn't work and steering us toward more effective strategies.

When we consider failure as a natural part of the learning process, then we can shift our approach and view it as an opportunity for success rather than a reason for discouragement. The wound caused by failure, when viewed positively, can fuel motivation, creativity, and innovation. This also compels us to explore new ways to solve our problems.

The perspective on failure differs from person to person. Some individuals take risks and see failure as part and parcel of life's journey, while others may have a more cautious approach. Though it is up to us to define our relationship with failure, we must not allow failure to cause us to fear, which can destroy the self totally.

Following is a speech given by Isabel Altamirano during an elocution competition at St. Thomas Aquinas Regional Secondary School in Vancouver, British Columbia. In this speech, she urges us to break down any negative thoughts. She also encourages us to dwell on our own strengths.

> Have you ever felt like you were drowning? I hit the water. The freezing shock is like a slap to my face, and I gasp. The water fills my Lungs, overwhelming, and it pushes me into the deep. My lungs are burning in the midst, sinking...
>
> In the surrounding ocean. I'm suffocating. I can swim, but the waves defy my desperate strokes. I reach upward, begging, pleading with the sea to let me breathe. Once more, my vision begins to darken. I drown too often. I wake up every morning at 5:30 and stumble out of bed, dizzy, exhausted, and out of my mind. There's a pile of clothing in the corner, unfolded, and worksheets scattered across the desk, and a little voice that welcomes me to the day. I

head toward the washroom, look at my reflection, and notice the voice has followed Me. With a single glance, I notice the flaws: the bags under my eyes, a tired, downcast look, the ragged breath escaping from my lips: imperfection after imperfection being listed off in my head like a shopping list. My mind starts racing as every mistake, every problem, every dent in my life is laid on me by that clear, persistent voice in my head. It's not an authentic voice, of course. It's just a thought, a glance at a mirror. It doesn't exist except in my mind. And along with the voice comes the thoughts of failure. You didn't eat yesterday? Failure. You argued with your siblings? Failure. You missed a practice? Failure. Look at this failed exam: you're a failure! This writing? It's nonsense. You're a failure. You missed the deadline, failure, failure, failure, Because that's all you are, a failure. You can't even hold yourself together for one day. You are nothing. You are nothing.

But is it true? Look around. At least one hundred twenty people in this room each have a voice in their heads telling them that they're not enough. Depression, anxiety, call it what you will—more than 20 percent of young people have darkness in them. And only 30 percent of those people are being treated professionally for it. Every twenty seconds, someone in the world loses their battle. It's hard to fight the voice on your own. I know it is. I know the feeling of failure, becoming the only identity in your life, and self-hatred becoming a constant burning sensation. I know what it's like to drown, to fight for your life, to come alarmingly close. As to losing, it's an entire war in itself, and you can't fight a war with only a single soldier.

An important person in my life once told me that there's a hidden pond somewhere, a pond where you can look at your reflection and be proud of the person on the other side, where you can say, confidently, "I'm talented, I'm valuable, I'm honest, I'm loyal, I'm authentic, and I'm a good friend," and no voice, no darkness, will shut you out. Chances are you're not at that pond yet—I know I'm certainly not—but it exists in the people around you. In fact, some people are at your pond already because they care for you, pray for you, and see you in a light that you don't. It takes time and it takes effort, but it's real. It's worlds more real than that baneful voice in your head. Three of the most dangerous words you can say to yourself are "I hate myself." One of the most hurtful things to hear in your own head is that you're a failure. And feeling like you're drowning? It's terrifying. But you have a voice too, and you can talk back. You can accept help from the people around you; you can seek it. You can make it to that pond and swim back to the surface, ignoring that voice.

In our silence, we must not let our failures grow like weeds within us, because otherwise they will whisper in our ears, "You mustn't give up." Thomas A. Edison put it this way: "Our greatest weakness lies in giving up. The most certain way to succeed is always to try just one more time."

Best Out of Broken

You must have heard the phrase *best out of waste*. This topic calls us to tweak it to *best out of broken*. Here is a recent example: The audience and the judges of *America's Got Talent* gave a standing ovation to Amanda Mammana for her mind-blowing audition. The nineteen-year-old Amanda suffers from a speech impediment, but she did not give up on herself. These were her words on the *AGT* stage: "As you can probably tell, I have a bit of speech impediment. It was definitely something that caused me to shy away and to hide. But I found that I don't stutter when I sing." She was the one who wrote the song for her audition. The lyrics of her song were based on the struggles she encountered throughout her life. "It's just about hard times, and if I could go back and change those things, I wouldn't, because they made me, me," she explains.

Here are a few of Amanda's lyrics from her audition song: "But what if I could go back in time/And change the way I felt about my life? /But then would I still have inside/Everything that brought me back to life."

This young girl's words are inspiring. Despite having a speech impediment, she sang from her heart. The striking words are, "If I could go back and change those things, I wouldn't, because they made me, me." We, not others, are the medicine for our own brokenness. This thought should encourage us to recognize the potential for positive change and transformation within ourselves, even in situations that seem dire.

Ultimately, the idea of *best out of broken* prompts us to shift our perspective and our approach, seeing challenges as opportunities for growth, innovation, and the creation of something better. It reminds us that in the most challenging circumstances, we have the potential to find beauty, strength, and a new beginning.

THOUGHT TO MYSELF

Brokenhearted, I sat in the corner.
All around me I saw people
Singing, dancing, playing music.
I thought, *I am a wasted body.*

The graduation party was in full swing.
I saw a teacher dragging a chair.
I got up, volunteering
To carry the extra chairs.

Someone tapped me on my back
And said, "I appreciate you."
I thought,
It's worth doing even the least thing.

Everything came to an end.
Some chose the finest professions.
I was not a doctor, a teacher, or lawyer material.
I thought, *This is my fate.*

Empty-handed, I stood.
My family placed some land in my hands.
I tilled it and harvested it
And planted fruits trees as the border.

My family witnessed life in the previously dead land.
The grains and fruits said it all.
They said, "He is industrious."
I said to myself, "Nothing is impossible."

Chapter 3

~

I Desire What Is Yours for Myself

I have my people whom I call my own. You have people whom you call your own. When you mention these people, you might call them "mine." We each have some people who are dear to us. Having them around and not accepting them as they are creates a hindrance to our own happiness. If we hold expectations or attempt to get others to become what we desire them to be, we may find ourselves in a state of dissatisfaction. These individuals can be our family members, relatives, colleagues, and so forth. When we are discontent with our dear ones, we feel a greater desire to have people other than our own in our lives. It is like thinking that the grass is greener on the other side of the fence. Sometimes, how a person appears does not tell the true story.

Everyone is aware that no one is perfect, not even I. It's harder to accept others' imperfections than to accept one's own. Appreciating and accepting others with their shortcomings is the least we could do to improve our relationships. When the people in my life are not perfect, I should not think that the people in your life will be perfect. It is futile to seek make others' loved ones my own.

Once, while conducting a retreat for prisoners, a preacher

posed the following questions: "What are your regrets in life? If given another chance, what would you change?"A few of them answered, "My wrong decision led me to be in this position." Many of them blamed their families of origin, and some of them blamed their spouses. It is sad that we blame others for our faults. Instead of blaming, we should divert all our energy into our own self-development. If we dig within ourselves, we will find that all the equipment we need for our development is available.

Allow me to share the sentiments of one of my friends. She lost her father when she was very young. From then on, her family lived hand to mouth. Her mom toiled day and night. She gave both her kids a decent education. She was open-minded and allowed her children to be involved in extracurricular activities as other moms would do in those days.

Now, when my friend looks back on her life, she says, "Though I was born and brought up in a marginalized family, I have no regrets about the family members I was given. I don't even blame God for our condition. I believe that I am the author of my own life. This thought kept me going."

She continued, saying, "My life was turned upside down when I fell in love with a man whose parents stole him from me. I was completely broken. Though many guys had their eyes on me, I showed interested in none of them, although in my culture, women should be out of the house and married by age twenty-five; otherwise, they are considered as a burden to their parents. I had no option but to marry a man who appeared handsome, but I failed to get to know his real self. Initially after my marriage, I wished I had my friend's husband. For quite some time, I longed for someone else's love to be mine. Over the years, I realized that I had to change my life and learn to accept my spouse with his limitations. Now I can say that in the beginning I had regrets, but later self-realization helped me to be happy with what I have."

When we desire someone else's loved ones for our own, we can never be content. We need to learn to be happy with our own people.

It is necessary to nurture the relationships we currently have rather than frequently yearning for others' loved ones.

Consistently desiring that someone else's loved ones be our own can lead to the cycle of comparison and envy. This can become an obstacle, preventing us from appreciating our own people with whom we have unique connections. We fail to recognize that each relationship is special and cannot be replicated.

The lack of active, positive interactions creates a chasm between us and our loved ones. This is the reason for the fading of mutual support and genuine care for each other. It is natural to be inspired by relationships that others have, but we should convert this into a fervent desire to have another person's loved ones for ourselves.

Except You

We use the phrase *except you* in a situation when we want to keep someone out of the group. This phrase can also have a positive connotation, but here we are focusing on the negative one. "Except you" simply means "I don't accept you." Yet at times, it is difficult to accept others as they are. This may not be true with our blood relations because, by default, they are a part of our lives. It is more relevant to the people who come into our lives, for instance, in-laws, coworkers, and neighbors. Unless we accept others with their imperfections, we cannot be at peace. It's difficult to accept others, especially when irrational thoughts push us to reject them. When we dislike others, it often stems from our own judgments, expectations, and predetermined notions. Our preformed ideas and beliefs about the people how other people should behave or conform to our standards can become an impediment to our accepting others. To cultivate the virtue of accepting others, we need to practice empathy and compassion. Sometimes putting ourselves in another person's shoes and learning to grasp his or her perspective can help to foster a sense of inclusion.

Embracing diversity can enrich our lives and broaden our understanding of human behavior. This does not mean we have to agree with or disagree with others' behavior, but we should acknowledge other people's worth and treat them with kindness and respect.

Most of us lean toward the cherry-picking strategy when we're choosing friends. The renowned companies have a policy of campus recruitment. There, they select the crème de la crème of the college. If we are the ones who may choose the team, then we would choose the players we like. For instance, where I lived, whenever we formed teams, two individuals were appointed as captains, and they had to select the players. They would first call out the players who played well and who got along well with them.

Let's take a look at Jesus's team of apostles. His method selection was not the same as our method of selection. Since he was holy and a perfect man, he could have chosen only holy people. But he selected individuals from different walks of life. Though he knew them through and through, he still chose them. Andrew, Peter, James, and John, by profession, were fishermen (Matthew 4:18; 4:21—these passages explain it well). Matthew was a tax collector (Matthew 9:9), and because of this, other people disliked him. Judas Iscariot was a thief, as John 12:6 says: "He did not say this because he cared about the poor but because he was a thief; as keeper of the money bag, he used to help himself to what was put into it." These are a few professions that are directly referred to in the scriptures. Jesus accepted everyone equally.

Steve Pavlina, a writer and motivational speaker, says, "I learned that accepting others and accepting oneself are two sides of the same coin; you can't love and accept yourself without doing the same for others." It becomes difficult for us to accept people we hate. Those whom we dislike, by hook or crook, we attempt to put them down.

Here is an apropos example: Jack and Toney were neighbors at home and classmates at school. Jack would get sick at the sight of Toney. Toney, not from a well-off family, knew his own limits. In the classroom, he would keep silent and read in the corner. The two boys' art teacher formed groups for a creative project. Jack was the leader of one group. Unfortunately, Toney was in his group. The task was a wildflower arrangement competition. Jack ordered all the other group members to pluck wildflowers and bring them to class. Since the land around Toney's house was full of greenery, he was able to grab some genuine wildflowers. The students who lived in the city purchased semi wildflowers. Obviously, they were fresh and gorgeous.

On the designated day, the clock was set for the students to arrange the flowers in vases. Jack was disgusted with the flowers that Toney had brought. They were tiny, yet pretty. To keep his reputation, in front of the group, Jack accepted the flowers with great hesitation. He arranged them toward the back of the vase just for the sake of placing them. He commented sarcastically, "I could not do any better because the uncivilized people brought literal wildflowers. If we are not announced as the winners, then you know who should be blamed."

When the results were in, Jack's group was awarded second place. All the team members were astonished at hearing the results, eager to know in which category they scored the highest marks. They learned that they had scored the lowest marks in arranging, which Jack had taken care of. To their surprise, they scored the most points in the authentic wildflower category. All of them appreciated Toney because he was the reason they bagged the prize.

Jack did not accept Toney, so whatever Toney brought or did was always wrong in his sight. When we dislike an individual, even if that person tries to be good with us, we cannot perceive what they are doing as good. This is because we see through our biased glasses and keep some people out of our circle of friends.

When we are reluctant to accept others in our lives, and then if an individual we are reluctant to accept appears in our lives, then we tend to blame that person for everything wrong that's connected to us. Even if the person may have caused no harm to us, still it is difficult for us to accept that person, maybe because we dislike his or her attitude or looks.

I believe that behavior differs from person to person. Thomas Merton says, "Saints are what they are, not because their sanctity makes them admirable to others, but because the gift of sainthood makes it possible for them to admire everyone else." We are called to love others. In Luke 6:31, Jesus says it all: "Do to others as you would have them do to you." We may not give the best to the people we dislike, but we can at least respect them, which they deserve.

Flame of Blame

The flame of blame burns the person doing the blaming. We think that blaming others for our pathetic condition will keep us secure. However, in doing this, we unintentionally create an encumbrance to our growth. The mayhem that emerges in us while we blame others burns our life's dreams. The flame of blame consumes us. We have no superpower to change others, but we can very well change ourselves. Instead of burning within because of others, we should burn our energy in the pursuit of making ourselves into better people. Blaming others is like washing our hands after painting but forgetting about the stains all over our shirt, which go unnoticed. Thinking, *I am clean,* after blaming others is like cleaning only our hands. In this, we avoid the responsibility of our own failures. Taking responsibility for our own failures empowers us. It enables us to acknowledge that we have the power to mold our lives, inspite of our external circumstances. It is futile to waste energy blaming others. It would be more productive to use that same energy to invest in self-reflection, self-awareness, and personal growth. This will help us to identify areas where we require improvement.

Blaming others may give us a temporary sense of relief. In the long run, however, it hinders our growth, and we end up blaming everyone in every situation. This is because when we engage in blame, we shift the focus away from ourselves and focus on the other person. It forces us to think that our successes and failures are dependent on others. This perspective leaves us powerless.

A few years ago, I was engaged in youth ministry, and there I came across Shawn, a youth who was gifted with arithmetic skills. He was the third of three siblings with two sisters and was from a lower-middle-class family. His dad toiled day and night as a refrigerator mechanic to raise the family. Shawn, being the only male in the family after his dad, was compelled to assist his dad. A neighbor commented that he was the chip off the old block.

Shawn's heart was somewhere else even after assisting his dad for six years. His daydreaming would make him absent-minded, decreasing his efficiency. His dad's insulting him in public, saying that he was indulging in woolgathering, scared him. His dad would even say that he, Shawn, was good for nothing. For Shawn to say anything to his dad was like getting blood out of a stone. "You are good for nothing." These discouraging words would repeat in Shawn's mind. As the years passed by, he gradually lost his self-confidence, to the point that he really thought he was hopeless and worthless.

When I met Shawn, his only complaint was, "My dad is the cause of my losing my buoyancy. When I see others with their dads, I feel jealous." He never got along with his dad. He wished he had a dad who allowed him to do what he liked and would keep him happy.

Who is to be blamed here, Shawn or his dad? His dad gave all his children a basic education. Shawn had a large opportunity to excel in math at school. His dad's behavior filled his mind with negative thoughts about himself. His dad's intention was to hand over the family business he had started to his son, wanting his son to have a secure future. If Shawn had come through with flying colors in his exams, his dad would have considered making him the owner of his business. Shawn kept thinking that his dad was exploiting him. If he had shown interest in the business, his dad would have offered him the job of bookkeeper. But Shawn was attracted neither to business nor to his studies.

Sometimes we have to adjust in life and accept the reality. Shawn's dad provided the children with basic necessities; not a single day passed without their having food. If Shawn thought his dad was wrong, then what about the children who are not privileged to have their basic needs met? Paulo Coelho states, "It's always easy to blame others. You can spend your entire life blaming the world, but your successes and failures are entirely your own."

When we blame others for our struggle, we will never be content. Even the trials that we are undergoing are right there before us. We must focus on the problem and know the people who are associated with it. If we continue blaming others, we will never learn and will never become who we were predestined to be.

Ludicrous Desires

It is human tendency to desire to have other people's loved ones when we are not happy with our own people. Such desires take us nowhere. To obtain contentment by filling the void within with others' loved ones is an untenable idea. It is a misconception that we can find satisfaction eternally, rather than addressing the core issues and working on our own growth.

The attempt to replace our own loved ones with those of someone else shows a disrespect for the uniqueness and autonomy of others. It forgets the importance of cultivating a genuine relationship based on trust and mutual respect.

Consider this story about schoolchildren. Teacher's Day was being celebrated, and the students had taken over the blackboard and chalk. When the cat's away, the mice will play. The classroom was like a marketplace. In calligraphic writing, Chris wrote his name and Sue's surname, which paper he stuck on the back of Sue's uniform. Everyone read it, "Chris Braganza," and had a big laugh.

Initially, Sue thought they were teasing her by calling her by Chris's name. She said to them, "It is obvious you're teasing me today because you have nothing better to do." Later she realized there was a problem with her back. She snatched the tag from her back and pounced on Chris. She pushed him, and then, in tears, she ran out of the classroom.

The teachers were chatting and laughing in the staff room. Chris and Sue's teacher noticed through the window that Sue was wiping tears from her face. With a tag in her hand, Sue walked toward the staff room. The teacher left her tea and rushed to her. After listening to Sue's story, the teacher called Chris. Sue brought him like a lamb for the slaughter, saying, "He is a bad boy."

The teacher, taking a breath, replied, "Dear, no one is bad. Everyone is good. However, what we do is bad."

Sue replied, "No, Chris does this to me always, and now it is too much."

The teacher put her hand over Sue's and said, "Yes, I understand. I say he is good because God created us in His likeness and image. But always remember, it is what we do that is wrong." Caressing Chris's back, the teacher said, "Dear, you guys are children. It is not the time to find girlfriend; it is time to study."

There was a history behind Chris's behavior. Eleven years had passed since Chris's birth, and most of those years he spent amid violence and abusive language. Though his parents had a love marriage, after Chris's birth, their marriage was on the rocks. Sharing responsibilities was a major issue. Since both parents were highly educated, neither of them was willing to bow their heads. Day by day, year by year, the situation became more aggravated and ended up in separation. In the bargain, Chris became like a nomad, spending one month with his mom and the next with his dad. He desired to have Sue's surname just to have parents like hers. He never liked to be in his own family.

Those words of his teacher, "He is a good boy, but what he has done to you is bad," changed his life. He understood that there was someone who loved him. Chris left behind his past and stepped into a new future.

We blame others for our growth, and sometimes the picture of someone else's parents blinds us, causing us to think that that person's parents are best for us. There are times when we, like Chris, wish we had been born in someone else's family. "It is my fate"; "Not me"; "My parents are responsible for my current situation"—these and many more complaints we hear from individuals who long to have some other person's family members as their own. Chris changed his mind and focused on making progress. As Anthony de Mello writes, "If it is peace you want, seek to change yourself, not other people. It is easier to protect your feet with slippers than to carpet the whole of the earth."

What Next?

Say we obtain the person we desire and that he or she becomes a part of our lives. What next? Here we are not talking about a woman or a man who wishes to marry someone else. We are talking about the people who already belong to someone else. Is it true that everything will be fine after the person you desire is in your life? If someone else's father becomes your father, it does not mean that he is going to change for your sake. Change comes from oneself and not from waiting for others to change.

Sometimes we may wish to be a part of an influential family. But sometimes being a part of a filthy rich family can lead us into vegetative mode, doing nothing and being nothing, and just being there. It is crucial to acknowledge that simply landing the person we desire, one with affluence and influence, will not ensure true happiness.

Moreover, the longing to be a part of a prominent rich family must be analyzed. It is essential to think twice about what motivates such an ambition. Is it a genuine personal conviction, or is it greediness for wealth? Becoming part of a prosperous family does not promise a person total fulfillment in life. It may lead to a stagnant existence if one relies on the possessions and privileges offered without making any effort. It can be the downfall of a person and all his or her pursuits.

Following is the story of an Indian mother-in-law who desired to have a perfect daughter-in-law, narrated by one of her cousins. In one traditional town, there lived a mother and her two sons. Ritu loved the behavior and nature of a girl in her neighborhood. She always imagined her older son marrying this girl and bringing her into the family as her daughter-in-law. Unfortunately, her older son fell head over heels in love with a colleague of his. Ritu's dreams were shattered. She was unhappy with her new daughter-in-law's way of life. The daughter-in-law was into fashion and beauty, whereas Ritu would do all the household chores. Ritu paid attention to only one part and titled her daughter-in-law "the spendthrift daughter-in-law." Ritu's gossip reached her neighbors' ears. Her daughter-in-law was having the time of her life at her son's expense. This was the story making the rounds.

Ritu had no doubt about what was beginning to cook in her younger son's heart. One fine day, he had to let the cat out of the bag because of pressure from his beloved. He said to his mother in pleasing voice, "I am going out with Nilam." This was the same girl whom Ritu was wishing her older son to marry. She was like a dog with two tails and had no words to say. She got excited to have the girl come over to her place as soon as possible. After a few months, the Ritu welcomed her second daughter-in-law with enormous joy.

The days passed, and the second daughter-in-law, Nilam, joined her job. The day's work and the bumpy ride on the bus drained her energy. Her spirit was willing, but her body was too weak to do the household chores. As the month passed, she neglected doing even the effortless housework. Ritu initially tried to close her eyes. At last she got fed up with Nilam. Ritu's second string of gossip spread like a wildfire among the neighbors. The neighbors said to each other,

"Nilam doesn't do anything at home, not even moving a single thing in the house. I feel for Ritu."

This example illustrates that even if we have the people we desire in our lives, we have to change at last and cannot expect them to change. If Ritu had appreciated the goodness of her first daughter-in-law, she would have been at peace. In the case of Nilam, Ritu emphasized her better side, but as time passed, she started to dislike her too.

It's Them

As individuals, we are indeed part of a community. The different elements of a community cannot be ignored. Rather, we have to learn to adjust to them in order to live. Community plays a vital role in an individual's holistic formation. But this does not mean that the community must be held responsible for any bad influence on the individual. As a person cherry-picks in other areas of life, here too one has to choose what is right and good for oneself. Everyone has the ability to make firm decisions and practice critical thinking, which releases a person from the clutches of the negative elements of the community. "It was them" should be the last thing we say when answering for one's own mistakes.

It is useful to adjust to the various elements of a community. Indeed, doing so is important for healthy coexistence. Individuals are expected to think of their values, dreams, and well-being while navigating their relationship with the community. This enables them to make choices that are in line with their own principles. It is vital to understand that a community consists of diverse individuals and that not every individual's perspective will be the same as ours. We may not like the approach of some people in the community, but this does not mean that entire community is evil. Each person has the choice to choose individuals as their companions, so blaming the community for one's own wrong choices makes no sense.

Cheryl writes an email to her friend after moving to another place of residence:

Hi, Ruth,

I hope you are hale and healthy. It has been a week since I have written to you. You do not know how much I miss the place and the people there. My dad's transfer to this ghetto, dirty, crowded area that has killed my dreams. I cannot see any ray of hope. This vicinity is not like yours, systematic and healthy. Here, with one gust of the breeze, the dust and garbage dances. The streetlights play hide-and-seek. Some are even broken and dead forever. Here, the roads have potholes, which inhabitants consider to be natural speed bumps. And don't ask me about my new school. Students arrive according to their own time, and teachers leave the class as they wish. It's a school with all colored students who are well versed in vulgarity. All these things hinder my intellectual and emotional growth. I am choked and discouraged from focusing on my goal.

I desire to have an elite and kind neighborhood as the one you are blessed with. It is a secure place to leave your house, even at midnight. I wish to have classmates of my same status where the language is refined and the interaction is enriching.

It is very painful to me to tell you that my life has gone from plus to minus. Negative thoughts have crept into my mind and clogged it. I really appreciate your concern for me in your last email. Thanks, and please do keep me in your prayers.

Sometimes we desire someone else's community as our own. Cheryl desired Ruth's community, which she thought was the best one. We often have a wrong conception of the society we live in. It is not others who make us what we are; it is we who form ourselves. Whatever our circumstances, we will have ample opportunities to emerge from them. This does not occur by chance but with hard work and commitment.

Someone rightly said, "Jesus loved sinners but hated sin." He walked and talked with the sinners but was not influenced by them. Matthew 9:9–13, Mark 2:13–17, and Luke 5:27–32 speak about the call to Matthew, the tax collector. Here, Jesus is seen dining with the community of tax collectors and sinners. The Scribes and Pharisees complained about his eating and talking with sinners. Jesus replied to them, "I have not come to call the righteous, but sinners to repentance" (Luke 5:32).

In Luke 7:36–50, Jesus is at a Pharisee's house for dinner. A sinful woman approaches Jesus, anoints his feet, and wipes the oil off with her hair. She leaves after kissing his feet. Jesus lets her go by saying, "Your faith has saved you; go in peace." The Pharisee who invited Jesus is astonished because Jesus allowed her to touch him. Other Pharisees questioned who it was who had given him the authority to forgive the woman's sins.

In Luke 19:1–10, Jesus is found at the home of a notorious tax collector, Zacchaeus. Though Zacchaeus repented and was a changed man, the Jewish leaders would not accept it. People who had seen Jesus do this began to grumble, "He has gone to be the guest of a sinner" (Luke 19:7).

These are some public interactions that Jesus had with sinners. Though he walked among the sinners, he did not sin. The sinners' community could not influence Jesus; rather, he influenced them with his love and compassion.

Let me tell you about a recent incident. One of my newly ordained priest friends is a sport enthusiast. He is blessed to pick up on any sport. His first posting as a priest was at the residence next to a sport complex, which was the icing on the cake in terms of his passion. His eyes were on the activities occurring in the complex. He learned that on every Friday, the youth played basketball. These young boys were not from the same college, same religion, or same age group, but were from the same vicinity.

One Friday, my priest friend approaching the boys and asked them to include him on one of their teams. At the drop of a hat, two of the Catholic youths said, "Good afternoon, Father." All the others got to know his identity and pretended to be good boys. It was because in their culture, a priest is highly esteemed.

A person's true colors come out when he or she is immersed in sports. After the match started, the polite words vanished and there was a string of vulgar words. The young priest was also a victim of this. But instead of reacting negatively, he responded with a smile. Above all, whenever he committed a fault, he said, "I am sorry." For a few weeks, this cycle of the boys firing bad words and the priest apologizing with a smile went on. Gradually, some players' behavior began to change. Especially when dealing with the priest, they shut their mouths.

When he told me of this incident, he said, "I enjoyed their company and was amazed to see a change in them. Even Hindu boys became friends with me and treated me with respect. And two of them are still in contact with me."

This young priest did not allow himself to be influenced by the boys. He did not even condemn them for their behavior. If he would have denounced them, they would not have allowed him to play with them. He remained neutral, but he responded with love. He simply focused on being good to them.

On many occasions, we waste our energy complaining about what others have done to us, and we forget what we can do for them. We can be kind even when others are rude to us. Our getting mad at them will not get us anywhere.

MAY YOUR LOVED ONES BE MINE

I desire your loved ones to be mine,
So I have become alien to mine.
Initially, with your people I felt fine.
Later, with both yours and mine, I did not feel fine.

Your loved ones may be appealing to me.
It matters, their appeal to me.
After having them in my life,
I thought I would get to stop making adjustments to my life.

This is not fighting for others;
It is fighting to steal loved ones from others.
It is loving the people around you,
Not desiring people who are not with you.

Whether yours or mine,
Everyone should be fine.
We are here to build a community.
Let not the community distort our thoughts' unity.

Happiness is looking into the eyes of one's own.
Happiness is accepting what is my own.
Happiness is not in blaming the family or society.
Happiness is in keeping my goal as my priority.

Chapter 4

~

I Wish for What Is Yours to Be Mine

The yearning to possess what others have is often driven by inequality. There is an enormous gulf between the haves and the have-nots in the present world. When a person faces such unfairness, the thought pops into his or her mind, I wish for what is yours to be mine. To some people, this is an inexorable thought. The consequence of this is obvious when a society's law and order is put to test. One of the Ten Commandments in the Holy Bible reads, "You shall not covet your neighbor's house. You shall not covet your neighbor's wife, or his male or female servant, his ox or donkey, or anything that belongs to your neighbor" (Exodus 20:17). A longing to have what others possess can lead to coveting these things. Sometimes it is better to be happy with what you have than to ponder on what you do not have. You can categorize the longing to have what others have by affluence, power, and position.

It is rightly said that money talks. Individuals speak louder when they have the backup of money and wealth. Comedian and actor Jackie Mason puts it this way: "Money is not the most important thing in the world. Love is. Fortunately, I love money." Since the world promises us the best prospects if we have wealth, subconsciously we desire to have what others have for our own. Affluence ensures us of the comforts of life, so who would like to be deprived of it?

It is important to acknowledge that while money buys comforts and opportunities, it does not ensure happiness. Studies have shown that when income increases, to some extent the bond between affluence and happiness declines. There are times when wealth is amassed at the expense of ethical values. Wealth is a means to an end, not the ultimate goal.

There is also a distinction based on white-collar and blue-collar jobs. White-collar jobs are considered professional jobs. They are office-based jobs that require higher education or specialized skills. Blue-collar jobs, on the other hand, are mostly physical labor. White-collar jobs most of the time come with a fat salary that contributes to stronger financial security.

The job we do enables us to increase our bank balance. It is not always a job, but the position at the job also matters. There are people who have two or three jobs just to make ends meet. And some people even go for odd jobs. Blue-collar workers face challenges in fulfilling their financial obligations and may be forced to take a second or even a third job. They become industrious in order to raise their standard of living.

We have to mind our thoughts when we hold multiple jobs at the same time. I am not saying that to be diligent, one must avoid all peccadilloes. Things slide into viciousness when one is led by greed. Hankering for money can lead to envy of others' positions at work. The person who is in the top position earns a fat salary. That causes a person with a lower profile to desire a higher position.

Authority and power both hold the potential for exploitation. An individual may exploit a position of power for purposes of individual gain and to manipulate others. Authority and power make the toughest jobs possible. The power dynamic sometimes leads to social inequality and suppression. Those with power can use power to spread discrimination and marginalization.

There are times when having power and authority can make an individual numb to the needs of others. Those who are in positions of power at times practice favoritism and ignore the best person for the job. The best examples of this sort of exploitation are most politicians, who have access to the best use of power when they are in positions of authority. They like to have power over others. Ask a person who is in power how difficult it is to let go of that power. Most of the people in power can get their jobs done through influence. If a person's life becomes easy when he or she is in power, then who would not crave power and authority?

Inhaling Inheritance

Blessed are those who are born with a silver spoon in their mouths, for theirs is the earthly kingdom. Inhaling inheritance means an individual is born into a rich family. The individual, by default, has everything on his or her plate and has his or her future secured. We should remember that wealth will come and go. Individuals who inherit a sizable amount wealth are bombarded with privileges and advantages. A broad range of opportunities are open to such an individual, helping him or her excel in life, which thereby leads to success.

It is important to ask yourself whether you use your wealth to uplift others or not. The true joy of possessing wealth is in building relationships by contributing the society. It is said that in giving, we gain, and that in amassing we lose. Sometimes in the race to amass wealth, we lose people, and sometimes through the good we do, we gain respect in the sight of others. In present times, the negative influence of affluence is more prominent than the positive influence. This leads to a fear of poverty. Hardly anyone realizes that smugness, egotism, lack of sincerity, rudeness, and so forth are the consequences of having riches. Most people would surely deny the fact that such negative vices are caused by money. However, money cannot provide perpetual happiness. It would be hard for wealthy people to believe that this is true.

Regrettably, in today's world, the negative influence of affluence is dominant. Some people who are born into affluent families develop a sense of arrogance and insensitivity. Their pride blinds them, leading to selfishness, rudeness, and bossiness.

Money is essential if one is to live a comfortable life. What matters is the attitude that people have toward wealth, as this is what impacts a person's character and behavior. Wealth can also be tremendous force for positive change if it is used maturely and with kindness. Acts of philanthropy, compassion, generosity, and so forth always bear fruits of justice and equality.

Imagine you notice a hundred-dollar bill on the sidewalk. Your first reaction is to be filled with joy. What would you do? Would you blow the hundred dollars on unnecessary pleasures? Or would you save it? Each person will use the amount in one way or another. Someone who is as poor as a church mouse may hold that hundred dollars in high regard, diligently considering how to make the best use of it. A poor person would think twice about which essentials to spend the money. In such a situation, the money will definitely bring temporally relief but will not take away any financial burden.

Someone who is rich would give little thought to how to spend the hundred dollars. Someone from a well-to-do family would have the liberty to spend that hundred-dollar bill however he or she so chose. Some may wish to spend it on purchasing luxury items or on pleasurable pursuits. Some may consider it to be peanuts and may donate it to a charitable association.

There is a vast difference between how various people handle money. A person who is not privileged will always have a desire to have money and wealth. But it is not good to paint all poor people with the same brush since there are many who are satisfied with what they have. Greed for money runs in the blood of many rich people. Even when they are blessed with wealth, they would not forgo an opportunity to increase it.

Whatever our financial status, it is counted as a virtue if we are content with what we have. Finding a life beyond material possessions is the key to satisfaction. We need to learn to appreciate our present situation, use our money responsibly, and make memories with others by using our wealth.

Finally, how we choose to spend money or wealth reflects our priorities, values, and personal status. It is nice to make deliberate decision to donate some of our money or wealth to charities that serve others.

Karl Marx's popular dictum on religion is, "Religion is the opiate of the masses." This dictum grants me the liberty to state that wealth is the opiate of the rich. According to Marx, religion is like opium (a drug), which dulls the senses and helps one forget the anguishes of the moment. In a similar way, religion pacifies people's consciences when they are suffering. Marx expected people to leave religion, God, and heaven behind. His intention was to create heaven on earth by establishing a good, equal society. Marx was a materialist and had no belief in God. He strongly believed in an equal society with no divisions. That is why he saw the hierarchy of religion as a major obstacle to promoting communism. He saw religion through his own lens but failed to understand it in the broader sense. It is religion that brings everyone under one umbrella, especially Christianity. This idea has its foundation in the scriptures. "The Spirit of the Lord is on me, he has anointed me to proclaim good news to the poor. He has sent me to proclaim freedom for the prisoners and recovery of sight for the blind, to set the oppressed free, to proclaim the year of the Lord's favor" (Luke 4:18–19); "Here is neither Jew nor Gentile, neither slave nor free, nor is there male and female, for you are all one in Christ Jesus" (Galatians 3:28). Religion also offers morality and values such as the importance of life, family, and community. Marx must have been unhappy with the organizational function of the church in his time.

Coming to the point, I restate that wealth is the opiate of the rich. When a person is obsessed with wealth, he or she turns out to be evil. Wealth becomes like opium, difficult to leave behind. It provides all the comforts of life, which leads the person to become selfish. In the bargain, the person's conscience dies. The wrong means of acquiring wealth do not prick at his or her conscience. The individual aims to acquire wealth by any means necessary, not much thinking about other people's emotions.

Karl Marx failed to see the goodness in religion maybe because of the condition of the religious hierarchies of his time. But instead of cutting one branch off the tree, he thought it would be better to cut down the entire tree. Wealth is good as it helps the individual to live a dignified life. We can use wealth in various ways, especially to uplift the marginalized, share with others, and bring a smile to others' faces. There are numerous philanthropists and responsible individuals who enthusiastically contribute to different causes and projects that are working toward a positive change in society. They know the power of wealth and use it for the well-being of the less fortunate.

It is sad to know that most wealthy people enjoy their money as a drug. They view wealth as a form of indulgence. It is obvious that many of them prioritize their own pleasure and materialistic pursuits over using their riches for the greater good. There is a phrase in Konkani, *Hanv mhaka, Dev somestank,* which means "I am for myself, and God is for all." This explains everything I'm talking about.

When the individual contemplates only wealth, he or she may be persuaded to think, *If I contribute to the greater good, then what about me?* This type of attitude leads to activities that break the law and disturb the social order. Theft is one of the consequences of desiring to have others' wealth. Here I am not talking about kleptomaniacs or people who steal in order to survive. This is about a person who desires to have the comforts of life that others have and who then robs others. Let me elaborate on this concept with an example:

At a renowned engineering college with a hostel attached, there lived students from different walks of life. The only thing they had in common was their excellent grades in their past schooling. Most of them were from wealthy families, and the others had taken out student loans to be there. The rich would show off, and the poor would see them.

Though Sam was from a poor family, he was highly intelligent. He would tutor some of the rich students, and with the money they paid him, he would pay his hostel rent. Ted was filthy rich. Because of the influence of money, he had been admitted to the college. Though his choice was to be a car racer, his parents wanted to see him become a mechanical engineer.

Sam would tutor Ted free of cost because it was conducive to tutor everyone in an unshared room like Ted's, which was accessible to many. On one occasion, Ted's parents gave him cash to pay for his college fees. It was mostly from their illegal business. On the following day, when Ted opened his drawer, he saw that the cash had gone missing. He broke out in a sweat and scurried to make a complain to the authorities.

No one knew who stole the money. The first suspect was Sam, because he was poor and was in Ted's room most of the time. The prefect started his search in Sam's suitcase, and there he found the cash. For a moment, Sam lost the respect of all his peers.

Sam denied having taken it, saying it was not his money. The prefect said, "Yes, it is not yours, it's Ted's."

Sam said, "No, please do not misunderstand me. That money belongs to Myron."

Ted said, "Please don't cook up stories of your own now. If you are in need of money, OK! You can keep it for yourself, but admit that you have taken from my room."

The prefect called for Myron. Without informing him of the details, he asked, "Did you give money to Ted to keep?"

Myron was a bit disturbed. "Yes!" he said.

The next question was, "Where did you get such a huge amount of money?"

Myron had no answer to it. He admitted that he was guilty.

Myron was a bon viveur, but he had parents with a weak bank balance. He had an eye on the expensive motorbike of a fellow student, John. Since Myron could not afford to buy one of his own, he sought opportunities to accumulate money. His desire for other people's things made him a thief.

The inclination to possess other people's belongings can stem from numerous things such as cultural influence, personal desire, competitiveness, or social pressure. It is obvious that we all have a desire to upgrade our standard of living and harvest the fruits of our hard work. Nevertheless, we should monitor this desire and prevent it from turning into an obsession for possessions. Things can also become very nasty when wealth is amassed at the expense of others, which harms both the perpetrator and the victim(s).

Even if we are underprivileged, it does not give us the right to steal. It is better to ask than to rob. This reminds me of my mother's words: "To rob is a shame, whereas to give is not shameful." We have a tradition during Christmastime of sharing our Christmas sweets with our neighbors and well-wishers. As kids, we would feel ashamed to distribute the sweets to these people. Our mother would keep her hands on our shoulders and say those words.

Scams and corruption are another problem, falling into the category of amassing wealth by deceiving others. People who engage in scams and corrupt practices believe that only wealth can bring total contentment in life. Other than adopting sincere ways, such people use unethical means to snatch other people's fortunes. Recently, I heard from a man who had received an email that said that he had won a prize of fifty thousand dollars. He was in seventh heaven. Without investing or giving it a second thought, he replied to the email. Immediately, he got a reply saying that he had to pay one thousand dollars to release the money and that the thousand would be refunded later. According to the guidelines, the man paid the money. He received another email telling him that this money could be only given in cash, so he should please transfer another two thousand for the security deposit. This money too would be refunded, he was told. The emails were so enticing that the man ended up paying another two thousand. Then he received another email saying, "Thanks, but there is a problem. For us to send the money to your country, you will have to pay tax to customs, around ten thousand dollars. This is the last step, then be sure that all the money will be yours." To make it somewhat genuine, they sent him a thousand dollars through someone as assurance. Without asking his son, he transferred the ten thousand.

Days and months passed, and there was no news from the agency. The man wrote email after email, but he got no reply. That made him realize that he had been trapped in a scam. Nowadays, such scams are very common, and we need to be smart.

The Joy of a Job

The joy of a job is the joy we gain from doing a job that we like. As the days pass, people's work ethic is changing. People switch to the job that brings in more income irrespective of whether it matches their God-given talents. Individuals risk their health, their family lives, and their spiritual lives to acquire wealth through a job. The competitiveness of the modern world has killed the joy of having a job. Indeed, the chase for income and affluence habitually takes precedence over job satisfaction and personal contentment. Preferably, a job should offer a sense of purpose and the opportunity to make use of one's talents. Finding career that aligns with one's zeal and passion can pilot the individual to a higher level of job satisfaction and better well-being.

This contemporary mindset causes individuals to crave a job that offers the best prospects. Getting someone else's job becomes a priority. Though the job may not be of a person's liking, he or she may like what it offers.

If we work without love, it can lead us to become slaves to money. When our aim is only to have wealth, then we become slaves to money. The aspect of love evaporates, and no joy remains in the job.

When a person aims to accumulate money through a job, he or she opens the possibility of turning into a monster. Vices such as jealousy, envy, and backbiting germinate in the person who restlessly desires to have another person's job. Envy emerges from the desire to have what others have. *Why is he [or she] paid more than me? I am doing similar work. Most of the time, I am much more efficient than him [or her]. I wish I had that job.* This is the outlook of the one who expects another person's job to make him or her more money. Here is another outlook: *I work day and night. I run all over the place. My job is tougher than his [or hers]. Why then is his [or her] salary the same as mine? I wish I had his [or her] job.*

Most Western women in the early and mid-nineties were homemakers, whereas the men were the breadwinners. Though sometimes what the men brought home was insufficient to run the household, they were satisfied with their jobs. In today's scenario, most individuals are educated and love to do their jobs. There is no harm in both spouses working. However, nowadays, the love for the job is drifting away, and love for wealth is being pumped in.

A dominant factor in our society is the emphasis put on financial well-being as a measure of success and social status. This approach can lead a person to crave a job with a handsome salary even if it does fit well with his or her skills and passion. The public mostly values external signs of accomplishment such as material things, social status, and earnings, which eclipse the relevance of personal contentment with one's job.

Here is a classic example: Luke was a cut above the average student. Medicine was not his cup of tea; it was his parents' pressure that had landed him in medical college. He had a flair for creative thinking, and he excelled at extracurricular activities. Taking initiative and keeping the ball rolling at college was his task.

Years passed by, and all Luke's comrades plunged into their respective endeavors. Luke's initiative led to the ribbon cutting of his own hospital. He became an employer, and he contacted his classmates to fill the job vacancies. The hospital was conducive to work, and the salary was high, adding to the bank accounts of his employees.

Mark from the start was sharp as a tack and was head of the class out of all the students in the entire medical college. One of his friends enticed him to join Luke's hospital because it offered better prospects. For Mark, it was humiliating to see Luke excel. His mind became restless. He would be satisfied only after seeing Luke's character assassinated—just because they had been neighbors and their parents were not on good terms.

Mark knew he was an all-rounder, and administration for him was a piece of a cake. He desired to take over Luke's hospital by proving he was brilliant and more capable than Luke. Mark was elated about the job that he was offered. It came with money, a prominent position, and the opportunity to take revenge, which was the icing on the cake. His eyes were on the money, and in the process he compromised his expertise in cardiology. On the other hand, Luke was focused on his future endeavors. Mark's efforts went in vain.

Mark was under the impression that he was better than Luke. Yes he was, but in studies, not in organizing. Luke was aware what was cooking in Mark's heart, but he believed in Paulo Coelho's words: "Never hate jealous people. They are jealous because they think you are better than them." Luke was aware of his and Mark's strong points. He did not react to Mark's desire to take revenge, instead responding by giving him the position just below his own at the hospital. Mark never expected that he would-be promoted within six months. He realized his mistake, and his respect for Luke grew in his heart. Mark's intention was a harmful his talent for conducting surgery was extraordinary. When he came to his senses, he concentrated on his abilities and not on the position and money.

Glory in Power

To feel gaiety upon obtaining power is to revel in power. Individuals love to be in positions of power, their spirits elated to have authority over others. The true self of any individual is seen when he or she is in power.

Some individuals in positions of authority are able to showcase their leadership and decision-making skills. For others, authority boosts their self-esteem and pride, which can be a treat for those working under them. There are some who are consumed by power, turning it into arrogance, unprincipled behavior, or disrespect for the well-being of others or their rights. This is called seeking glory in power.

Glory in power can also be seen when people utilize their power to influence and to bring about positive change, uplifting society and its citizens. They use their positions of responsibility and power to make the world a better place to live.

Abraham Lincoln said, "Nearly all men can stand adversity, but if you want to test a man's character, give him power." If power gives one authority over others, then who would like to let go of it? Individuals holding high positions in government or in corporations at times find it difficult to let go of those positions.

Power in itself is not evil. Someone has to be in power to run any firm smoothly. A renowned corporate leader puts it this way: "I am not fascinated in power for power's sake, but I'm interested in power that is ethical, that is upright, and that is good for all." Power can be used for the betterment of others or for the betterment of oneself. By and large, most individuals in power exercise that power for their own benefit. People long for the power that others enjoy so that they can have individuals under their thumbs.

Here is an example of seeking power: Many moons ago, there was a king in India who was a philanthropist. He was a people's king, as he had no crown. His late father had lost a war, and in the commotion, his crown had gone missing. There was a rumor in the air that the crown was hidden somewhere in the kingdom, but no one knew the exact place.

There lived a farmer who was as poor as a church mouse. His name was Gurma. One morning, it was raining cats and dogs. Gurma thought it was the best day to till his land. With the pristine water from above and the mucky water from below, without Gurma's knowledge, the ox pulled the plow over the furrows. The plow got stuck into the ground. On hearing a metallic sound, Gurma swiftly knelt down. Seeing metal, he took a closer look and noticed that there were precious stone stuck in it. To his surprise, it was the lost crown of His Majesty. Gurma, being as honest as the day is long, went and handed the crown over to the king without expecting anything in return. The magnanimous king awarded him with an enormous mansion and the topmost position in his court.

The ministers in the court were jealous. Suraj, the minister in charge of the northern detachment of soldiers, had his eyes on Gurma. Suraj was hungry for power. He was a sadist and enjoyed making others pay and suffer. He also loved to steal other people's thunder. After a year, Suraj could not see Gurma excelling. He desired Gurma's power and authority. Now Gurma was fixed in that position, so it had gone from Suraj's hands. He directed his thoughts and actions toward impressing the king and undermining Gurma. He knew that the king was easy to deceive.

One fine day, Suraj approached the king with a complaint about Gurma, saying to him, "My Majesty! I shouldn't say this, but I am helpless. Do you know that Gurma is doing black magic on you?"

The king asked, "What makes you say that?"

"I will tell you, but I want you to promise me his position in the court." The king reluctantly agreed. "He performs his magic in his old hut. Every morning without fail, before coming to the palace, he visits his hut. The darkness creeps into that hut at night and leaves only after his visit. If he loves the hut so much, then why doesn't he renovate it? Your Majesty, if you think this is a lie, then come and see it tomorrow morning."

The king agreed to go with Suraj the following day. When the two were watching, out of sight, Gurma, after descending from his horse, walked straight into his hut. The king raised his eyebrows at the sight. Gurma stayed in the cold, clean hut for approximately ten minutes. The king made a hostile move toward the palace, telling Suraj to bring Gurma to see him as soon as possible.

In the presence of all the ministers, the king interrogated Gurma as to the mystery of his early morning visits to the hut. Gurma responded, "My lord, I go there to make myself aware of my past. Every straw of the hut whispers to me, reminding me of who I was and now of who I am. This enables me to remain humble. If I renovate the hut, then the purpose will be lost." The king appreciated Gurma's motive and banished the envious minister.

This king is a great example of a person who uses the power for the sake of others. Suraj is a man who longs to possess another person's power. In this life, it is best to be happy with the power we have. If power is given to us, then that is a different story. If it is grabbed from others, then that is a sign of selfishness. Power has a tremendous ability to tempt and provides a sense of success. This leads to dictatorship. True contentment and self-understanding come from a holistic approach that includes personal growth, genuine relationships, and a broader understanding of the motive behind obtaining power.

LAUGHS!

The poor desire to talk wealth,
But the rich hold it tight till death.
The best treatment is promised by wealth,
But it doesn't promise excellent health.
Wealth laughs at the greedy and says,
"You will leave me here on earth."

Pride pushes humility away when one is in a high position.
Humility stomps on pride when one is in a low position.
Pride wins when a position possesses an individual.
Humility wins when a position teaches an individual.
The position laughs at the covetous and says,
"You will be kicked out one day even from the top position."

The powerful commend and dominate.
The powerless bow and supplicate.
The powerful feel as if they are walking on the clouds in the sky.
The powerless feel stuck in the muddy pie.
Power laughs at the avaricious and says,
"You will be feeble and will be deprived of all power."

PART II

Introduction

Part two seeks to persuade you to smile with others. It encourages you to perceive the others in your life as a blessing. Its theme is about becoming wise and laughing when I make the mistake of comparing. Shaking others' hands is a sign of acceptance irrespective of how they are different. Giving a round of applause to others for their hard work is an acknowledgment of their talents. Indeed, saluting others for their achievements is a sign of humility. You achieve inner happiness by accepting others as they are and living with them with a right attitude of adaptability.

The last chapter of part two discusses ultimate dependence on God Almighty. Its theme is about having a strong belief that we exist because He exists. To rely on God is to begin all over again each day as if nothing has been done and yet there is much to learn. The journey to our final destination is energized by the hope provided to us by the Almighty.

Chapter 5

~

I Love All You Are

To make the world a better place to live, we ought to accept everything as it is and coexist with other people without prejudice. The sun shines on all people alike. What makes the difference is *us*. We have the choice to stay in darkness by covering ourselves and shielding ourselves entirely from the sun, which is a metaphor for purposefully disconnecting from people who are different from us whom we do not consider to be part of our inner circle. This rude act of exclusion is motivated by selfish desires.

As the sun's rays brighten every corner of the earth, we should open our hearts to accept every individual regardless of caste, creed, color, race, religion, nationality, or gender or any other feature that separates us as people. The sun is like humanity, and it is beyond any discrimination. We human beings sometimes favor and care for only those who belong to us. Let every corner of our hearts be brightened by the rays of acceptance.

Human beings have the ability to extend understanding and accept everyone despite each other's differences. Fostering a welcoming nature, we can build a community that celebrates diversity in unity. This is done by recognizing the innate worth of every person and respecting everyone alike. One has to constantly confront one's own biases, broaden one's horizons, and learn to treat others with respect and kindness. The journey of welcoming all under the same umbrella is a collective endeavor that demands the contribution and commitment of every single individual.

My Soul Delights in the External

The human soul delights in others' outward appearance, values, and beliefs. A person accepts another person as an original copy from the core of himself or herself. Appreciating and accepting others as they are from the roots of one's being is like watering all the plants in the garden of human creation. Such a nurturing atmosphere enables individuals to articulate themselves genuinely, without fear of being deserted and judged on the basis of their differences. One should seek to create an environment where one feels secure amid others' presence. Other people's size, color, creed, gender, status, and looks become irrelevant when one sees them through the eyes of equality. These exterior features and personal choices fade away in the light of distinguishing the inherent worth and dignity of every person. One's own imperfections and those of others fit together and form a cohesive whole. Being a jack-of-all-trades and master of none leads a person nowhere. Yes, a person may be a jack-of-all-trades, but still he or she requires others' assistance in other spheres of life. By valuing others from the heart, one creates an environment where people feel safe and secure.

Features Deceive

Unity in diversity. Sometimes this phrase remains as a utopian idea in the real day-to-day life of a human being. People of all walks of life and with many different origins living in peace enhances society, although this may not be true in every case. Physical appearance is just an accident; in essence, we are all *Homo sapiens.* Our entire focus should be on our commonalities rather than our dissimilarities. This can cultivate a sense of oneness and build an inclusive world where everyone is encouraged to thrive using their God-given talents.

It is important to keep in mind that physical appearance is purely an external feature and not some foundation for justifiable discrimination or chauvinism. By transcending these peripheral aspects, we can come to appreciate the richness that every person contributes to the human experience.

"What spirit is so empty and blind that it cannot recognize the fact that the foot is more noble than the shoe, and the skin more beautiful than the garment with which it is clothed?" is a question asked by Michelangelo. Blooming flowers exhibit a mind-blowing array of colors in the garden. Those same colors make more of an impact when they are placed in bouquet with other flowers. When the flowers dry, all the colors fade. A bouquet is beautiful when the flowers are fresh. Similarly, we need to beautify our lives when others are with us and not when they are gone.

Let me compare the human external self with a national soccer team. The very fact that the individual is on the national soccer term acknowledges the fact that he is a player with an innate talent for playing soccer. As a team, the members are strong. If a player is short or from a different ethnicity, it does not matter as long as he plays well. We could make a comparison to our five fingers. They are each a different shape and size, but all are equally important to us for doing our day-to-day work.

Esteem Cultures and Creeds

Others' creed and culture is not a thorn that gets in the way of my life but is the light along my way. Whether we are Hindu or Muslim, Christian or Jewish, our human features remain the same. Others' beliefs are our inspiration when doubts arise in our minds about our faith. We encourage the various diverse creeds and cultures by accepting them as they are. When we do this, we gain a deeper appreciation for the immense tapestry of human experience and the expression of holiness. This can reinforce our own faith by triggering us to reflect, inquire, and seek a better understanding. Instead of pushing away the various religious beliefs, we should approach them with an open mind and heart and with a readiness to learn. This will help us to have a healthy dialogue, foster mutual respect, and gain the opportunity to discover common ground among the various faiths and cultures.

I know of a young man who was born and brought up in India but who works abroad. After having stayed in a foreign country for a couple of years, he went for the holidays to India. When he returned after the holidays, he had turned over a new leaf in his faith life. Without fail, he was seen every Sunday for the Eucharistic service. When he was asked what made him change his perspective toward religion, he said, "When I came to this country, observing the attitude of people toward their faith, I drifted away from my own faith. My spiritual life went to dogs. This time I visited Mumbai, India, during my vacation. It was my first trip back after five years. There I experienced the current of faith in other religions. I noticed Muslims sitting on the streets to pray three times in a day, and Hindus solemnly celebrating their various feasts by decorating and illuminating their houses. I could see these things since I was in a large metropolitan city. In my village it is another story, as there the people are of only one faith. This made me realize that people of different faiths believe in the divine, which enabled me to strengthen my faith in Jesus." He paused. "Their faith saved mine." This young man's story of how his faith was strengthened by encountering people of other religions opens the opportunity for everyone to seek what their religion has in common with other religions. It is safe to say that, in one or the other, the various faiths are interdependent, which gives us a broader understanding of religion.

Seeing others engaging in an intimate relationship with God encourages you to return to your faith after having gone astray.

Whether you wear saffron, green, or white, your garments just cover your skin but do not change its color. Those colors may project your religion, but they should not hold you back from becoming friends with other people. Whether you apply tilak in the morning or apply ashes to your forehead on Ash Wednesday, and whether or not you wear a white skullcap while praying, you are still considered brother or sister. Mahatma Gandhi says, "The need of the moment is not one religion, but mutual respect and tolerance of the devotees of the different religions." I believe that you and I can live peacefully in this God-given world.

Different cultures are the spice of life. I am from Goa—India. The state of Goa has a culture that is altogether different from that of the other states of India. Its culture is a blend of Portuguese and Indian. When I considered my years in Goa, I got the feeling of having been in a smaller bubble. This compelled me to think that the way of life in Goa is the ultimate way and that I could not swallow the truth outside my culture. Though I had seen other parts of India on TV, I was not yet convinced that they existed in real life.

I continued my studies in Mumbai, a metropolitan and multicultural city—also a business hub. People from various states of India had flocked to the place for better prospects. Now my only cultural bubble had been joined to another bubble: a multicultural society. I came across people who followed customs and traditions that were very different from mine. I was dipped in colorful Indian culture. In such a multicultural environment, to say that mine is the only true religion is like walking on thin ice.

A few years after that, I was transferred to Vancouver, British Columbia, in Canada. Canada is a young, developed country flooded with immigrants. There I encountered international cultures. Some of the people practiced the same faith, yet it was different according to culture and tradition. I did not notice this much at the national level. Initially, it was a culture shock for me, as the difference between my former way of life and this new way of life was like the difference between night and day. I felt I had been thrown from a pond and into an ocean of cultures. As the days and months turned into a year, I developed a knack for living with people from diverse cultures.

All three of the foregoing experiences broadened my horizons. I could compare my journey to a frog in the wall. The frog jumped out from the wall and found itself in a pond. Now its space had increased and it had a lot of room to go about in. One day, in pursuit of better prospects, the frog leapt and landed in an endless river that emptied into the ocean. Now the frog was free to move and grow. It also enjoyed the company of an array of marine life.

Like the frog, we too have to learn to accept others' cultures and ways of life. There is beauty in every culture. Embracing people of other cultures and rejoicing with them is the secret to a happy life. Every culture has its own unique customs, rituals, language, arts, and distinct way of living. When we admire and appreciate the features of other cultures, it broadens our worldview. In immersing ourselves in other cultural experiences, we are endowed with a new perspective and are able to form a profound image of humanity. Interacting with the people of various cultures provides us with new ideas and experiences. It helps us to pull down the walls of misunderstanding and build bridges of understanding.

Rejoicing in the diversity of cultures enhances the warmth of unity and harmony. Our differences do not cover the vast carpet of humanity where we all share common values, morals, and virtues. Different cultures encourage us to step outside our own cozy world and face the challenges brought about by differences. Acceptance of people of other cultures opens the gate to new friendships, enculturation, and collaboration.

Revere Those Who Are Least in Terms of Status

Rather than being first or last in status, it is best to seek to be the kindest. Your social status is not a step for me to climb up. However, it does open my eyes to acknowledge that there are people who are in need of my help. Whether we are rich or poor, what endures are our good works.

In this world, social status often speaks of an individual's worth. It is important to know that the true value of a person comes not in his or her material possessions or social reputation but in how he or she relates with others. Instead of using others' status to ridicule them, one must learn to appreciate the intrinsic beauty in every individual's way of life.

Benevolent gestures and good works are not rooted in one's status. Poor people and rich people each have the same ability to make a positive impression on others with their simple words and actions.

Our social status is like a shadow. When we are with the people who are higher in status than we are, things are more vivid, as if light has just been shined into the shadows. We feel uncomfortable like a fish out of water, conscious of our every movement. No light and no shadow is the situation when we feel comfortable among people of the same status or a lower status and we go unnoticed.

A.P.J. Abdul Kalam says, "Empty pockets teach you a million things in life, but full pockets spoil you in a million ways." Sometimes, status does not come to a person's rescue. Being of a lower social status prepares an individual to be tough and face the unpleasant moments of life in the future.

Let us throw some light onto this topic with the help of the play *Pygmalion* by Irish playwright George Bernard Shaw, who titled this play after the Greek legendary figure. In ancient Greek mythology, the character Pygmalion falls head over heels in love with his own ivory sculpture, *Galatea*. The goddess of love infuses life into *Galatea*, a circumspectly carved woman. At last, Pygmalion and Galatea tie the knot.

In this play, Shaw portrays the journey of a lower-class peasant woman who becomes a duchess. In the play, Professor Higgins, a linguist of Indian dialects with proficiency in phonetics, tells Colonel Pickering that he will transform a Cockney-speaking

Covent Garden flower girl, Eliza Doolittle, into a duchess who speaks fluently. Pickering promises Higgins that he will bear the expense of the experiment if Higgins indeed transforms Eliza and passes her off as a duchess at an upcoming party. Eliza is convinced to take the lessons in phonetics to polish her language skills and become a refined lady.

After several months of intensive practice, the first trial is at Higgins's mother's home. There are a few guests, including Freddy, who admires Eliza and had fallen for her. Eliza makes a great impact on the people around her through her posture and pronunciation. Everything is going well, but when Mrs. Eynsford mentions influenza, a problem arises. This reminds Eliza of her aunt, who died of the disease. She becomes emotional and reveals some personal facts, such as her father's alcoholism. This behavior is not becoming of a duchess. Her vocabulary goes haywire. Though her pronunciation is good, the content of her speech is not acceptable at such a gathering. That day, she made a narrow escape.

This situation is important for us to reflect on. Yes, we need to change for the better, but sometimes we cannot prevent the interference of our core self. We may wish to belong to a higher class, perhaps because we have an industrious attitude, just as Eliza pretended to be what she was not. Nevertheless, reality overwhelms us when we get caught up in emotion.

Later in the play, with the training now over, Eliza has to pass a second test. She is taken to an elite party where she performs superbly and deceives everyone into thinking that she is a distinguished lady. The trouble occurs when the experiment is over. Eliza is caught between two choices: whether to leave everything and go back to her old way of life or to remain in her present state. She questions her existence, asking herself, *What is my status in society?*

Higgins, having become accustomed to Eliza, takes her for granted. He does not give her the respect a duchess would deserve. Eliza has feelings for Higgins, but seeing his insulting behavior, she swallows her emotions. As a courageous and self-determined woman, she departs from his house. When the play ends, the spectators are not sure whether Higgins will win Eliza's love or if she will go with Freddy, who loves her more than anything.

In the sequel to *Pygmalion*, Shaw insists that Eliza should not marry Higgins because of their age difference. In the epilogue, Shaw provides information about Eliza's marriage to Freddy. Economic constraints were a main concern since Freddy had no money and no job. His status and dignity had both been reduced by marrying a flower girl from a lower class. Freddy had dashed his mother's hopes that he'd marry a woman with a huge fortune. Eliza, too, had no help from her selfish father to marry. At last, the colonel offered some amount of money to the couple to marry. Later, they opened their flower stall and lived happily ever after.

Social status is a highly evident theme in this play, which sheds light on what it is like to be born into lower-class family. Eliza, as a flower girl, looked down on a street corner in the city. When she first came into contact with Higgins, he disrespected her because of the way she spoke. His disrespect for her continued even after she had learned to speak well. The man who deserves praise is Freddy, who truly loved Eliza. He gave up his social status just to be with her. Love ignores all the barriers of status. Someone said it right: love is blind.

Within the community, status may create partitions and hierarchies that mirror those of the society at large. But status is a barrier that we can overlook easily if we so wish. Perhaps we are unable to show love every time, but we can have mercy. Love has a tremendous ability to cause one to transcend one's social status and bring him or her together with others. Love has the capacity to melt hearts and allow people to be with one another beyond the walls of status. Love enables us to jump over the hurdle of social label and approach others with compassion.

No Person Is an Island

We all are interdependent. Our interconnectedness is a primary element of the human experience and the world in which we live. We rely on each other for our various needs. Others support us, and collaboration is essential to add comfort to life. Whether we are associated with loved ones or colleagues, or even with an unfamiliar person, we depend on each other in various ways.

We are dependent on others, both individuals and society as a whole. At the personal level, our well-being is enhanced by our relationships with others and the support they provide. We count on others for companionship, for a shoulder to cry on, and for help in times of trial. No one is completely self-sufficient, and interactions with others mold our personalities and contribute to our well-being. At the community level, such interdependency is obvious when we look at the complex web of liaisons and arrangements that sustain communities, for example, laws and regulations that assist in keeping the peace. We may be closely associated with the professionals who toil day and night to fulfill our needs and provide us with necessary services. For instance, farmers dirty their hands to feed us; health-care workers take our temperature to determine if we are ill; and educators educate the future generations with skill and knowledge. As we are related to each other, our every action and choice matters, and in turn, others' actions and choices matter too, for we influence each other on our way to achieving contentment in life.

Our dependence on others leads to sense of compassion, sympathy, and concern for one another and the world at large. Close relationships with others encourage us to make this world a better place to live in. We must always keep in mind that we are not isolated individuals, but a part of the larger humanity, and our decisions ripple outward and influence others.

Following are a few lines of John Donne's poem "No Man Is an Island":

No man is an island, entire of itself;
Every man is a piece of the continent,
A part of the main.
If a clod be washed away by the sea, Europe is the less.
As well as if a promontory were,
As well as any manner of thy friends
Or of thine own were.

Donne, in this metaphysical poem, makes a comparison between a man and an island. An island is a landmass existing apart from any mainland. According to Donne, no man can exist without other human beings, which idea he puts forth in the phrase "entire of itself."An individual is incomplete without others' assistance. "A piece of the continent" means that every person is like a portion of the mainland, that is, humanity. Donne uses the word *clod*, which has the two meanings: a lump of earth and an unwise person. He states that if a lump of earth is washed away, it will be a loss to the mainland. In a similar way, every person, even an unwise person, is important to humanity.

In this poem, Donne shows the importance of community to the individual and of the individual to the community. Though everyone's contribution may not be the same or effective, it is essential to the community. As in chess, every piece has a role to play, even a pawn, which is insignificant but also may move to protect the king.

Gratitude for Aptitude

Having gratitude for others' aptitudes leads us all onto the path of encouragement. By acknowledging and appreciating the talents of our fellow beings, we create an environment that fosters cooperation and mutual growth. This promotes a culture of enriching each other by celebrating others' strengths.

Vocalizing our gratitude for others' aptitude also helps to

inculcate the virtue of humility within us. Humility enlightens us with the wisdom that everyone has one or more of a vast web of skills and aptitudes and that no single person possesses all the aptitudes under the sun. It is good to recognize the value of diversity and the contributions that each individual makes. Sincerely acknowledge the talents and skills that others share with us and with society at large.

No one can say, "I am independent." Even our births depended on our parents. I like to put this idea this way: "My life without you." What would my life be like if you did not supply me with vegetables? What would it be like if you stopped providing eggs, milk, meat, etc., for a day? What would be my day like without electricity? I would be handicapped with no internet, elevator, air conditioner, heater, etc. What would my days be like without any entertainment? What if you did not come to work for a day? Who would cook and clean my house? Domestic workers are as important to those they serve as are the workers to a company. What if you were to discontinue performing your professional job? Who would treat my illness or fight my case in court?

Each person's talent is a gift to others. Farming is a talent, for example. Not everyone is gifted with a green thumb. Animal husbandry is also a gift; not everyone is able to take the risk of rearing animals. Not everyone has the genius to discover and invent. Not everyone has the gift of gab or an ear for music. Not everyone is blessed with the ability to make people feel cheerful and relaxed or to make people laugh, cry, etc. not everyone is a smart enough cookie to have a profession such as doctor, teacher, or lawyer. Everyone you see around you uses their talents for your comfort and growth. Then why should you be jealous of them? Here I would like to quote the French novelist Marcel Proust: "Let us be grateful to people who make us happy; they are the charming gardeners who make our souls blossom." Yes, others are the gardeners of our lives. With their talents, they nurture us.

Here I will relate an incident involving a woman named Nora, the nightingale of our parish. On one Palm Sunday, the church was magnificently decorated with palms. It was not colorful but was elegant since it was the season of Lent. I was all set for the celebration with palms in my hand. Nora came to me to discuss the liturgy. I said, "Take it easy. You will do well." She is a woman with a golden heart. Though she had played the piano and sang in the church choir for decades, she remained humble throughout.

She replied, "Yes! I get all the glory. Those who need it, they don't get it." She spoke what was on her heart concerning the church's decor. She admitted that everyone appreciates her for her talents, which the public can easily see. She was sad for those who did a lot behind the scenes who were not acknowledged. She especially felt for the ones who had decorated the church.

We should learn to appreciate others' talents. Nora's words of concern remind me of something Plato wrote: "A grateful mind is a great mind, which eventually attracts to itself great things." Nora remained grateful to all who had toiled to celebrate Palm Sunday.

To appreciate others' talents is a priceless skill that can significantly boost our relationships with other people and cause us to become instrumental in their personal growth. The appreciation assists in forming an accommodating an environment where all can look for the opportunity to thrive in their own respective fields. For our part, we should take time to acknowledge others' God-given gifts and celebrate others' unique talents that contribute to the well-being of society.

Rejoicing in Others' Glory

Rejoicing in others' glory is a marvelous and honorable quality that reflects a munificent and altruistic mindset. This includes experiencing genuine happiness and rejoicing when others succeed or achieve certain milestones. Instead of feeling jealous, envious, and bitter about others' accomplishments, we are called to rejoice genuinely and applaud others' achievements. When we rejoice in others' achievements, we, in return, help ourselves. It keeps our mind free from fear of failure. By celebrating others' achievements, we realize that successes and failures are temporary. Today, you may be the winner. Tomorrow, I may be the winner. What is important is how we take it. We have to ask ourselves, "Do I take my win with pride? Do I take my losing as failure?"

Rejoicing in another person's glory can promote a communal environment, reinforce relationships, and establish an accommodative condition to live peacefully. The positive atmosphere caused by rejoicing in another person's glory inspires others to do the same. Healthy competition, collaboration, and encouragement are some of the outcomes of rejoicing in others' glory, which allows us to find joy in our own achievements. This gives us a positive perspective on life.

The credit for achievement goes to hard work. When an individual performs well with his or her God-given gifts, others too should rejoice. It is good to inculcate the positive attitude of *I can't do that, but at least I am good at other things.*

Here is a story about a young man who was known as "Pulley Boy" at seminary. Pulley Boy was a content lad. Annually, the seminary would stage four to five programs. This provided an opportunity for young, talented seminarians to showcase their God-given talents. In the olden days, the curtains were pulled up after every scene. The pulley boy was faithful in doing his job. He was the only one whose role in the annual stage program never changed. One of his companions, who had a soft spot for him asked, "Roy, do you not feel bad that everyone calls you Pulley Boy? If you wish, I can give you a small role in the play I am directing."

Pulley Boy said, smiling, "No, thanks! Acting is not my cup of tea. I love my job. I don't mind what others say about it. I believe I too am important. By not pulling the curtain up, I can make them wait." Pulley Boy had no regrets. He enjoyed watching others perform on the stage. Upon every successful program, he rejoiced with others without any hurt feelings.

Jesus's Blueprint of Love

"Jesus's blueprint of love" refers to the teachings of Jesus Christ. He was the paragon of love. In the Bible, he is considered to be the embodiment of divine love and is the model for all believers. His acts of compassion and mercy are signs of his love beyond measure.

"All this took place to fulfill what the Lord had said through the prophet: 'The virgin will conceive and give birth to a son, and they will call him Immanuel (which means "God with us")" (Matthew 1:22–23). For people of other faiths, it is incomprehensible to think of God taking the form of a human.

Jesus showed love through his actions. He was compassionate toward the marginalized, forgave the sinners, cured the sick people, and reached out to the Gentiles, all of which he did with love. He commanded his disciples to love even their enemies and to pray for those who persecuted them. He treated everyone equally and told his disciples to treat others as they would like others to treat them.

Jesus stressed the importance of selfless service. The type of service that he said was acceptable for his disciples was service without reciprocation, that is, with no gain in return. He washed the feet of his disciples and thereby set an example of humility and selfless service, which is also called "servant leadership, "a type of leadership that calls followers to love, not only those who love them, but also those who are different from them and are difficult to love.

Philippians 2:5–8 rightly expresses, "In your relationships with one another, have the same mindset as Christ Jesus: who, being in very nature God, did not consider equality with God something to be used to his own advantage; rather, he made himself nothing by taking the very nature of a servant, being made in human likeness. And being found in appearance as a man, he humbled himself by becoming obedient to death—even death on a cross!" Jesus is the example of ideal love for the poor, the Gentiles, sinners, the human race, and the entire world. He treated everyone equally.

BREATH

The tall coconut trees smiled at every laugh of the waves.
The birds intently communicated to the fishermen's cast-offs.
I sit alone inhaling and exhaling to the beat
of some transcendental music.
The blown sand dancing with the wind kisses
my lips, and my tongue peeps.
That saltiness cracks open my jaw to spit and my eyes to see the sea.

I saw a blonde woman clapping her hands; it looked
to me that she was dancing on drugs.
With disheveled hair, and panting for breath, she
raced to men in turbans with bushy hair.
All sprinted in the opposite direction, but she
came and stared at me. I ignored her.
A Chinese man intentionally pushed me. I
smiled and pulled out my ear buds.
I said, "Excuse me! Am I in your way, or are you
in mine?" He pointed toward the sea.

Oh! Realizing where I was, I exclaimed, "How did
I miss seeing the child being engulfed?"
I made my way in haste, and I jumped into the surf,
but the wanderers and tourists grumbled.
That woman was the child's mother. Pounding her head on an
unknown shoulder, she cried. A nurse and a teacher said, "How
we can help?" but everyone were waiting to hear his breath.
Unconsciousness stole the mother's breath, so
all the comforting words went unheard.

I stayed stunned; calling on the gods of the universe was the last resort.
With my heart beating louder, the suggestions deafened my ears.
The slightest sign of the child's breath would ease our heartbeats.
People of all walks of life came and added to
the circle. No barriers hindered them.
Then the puff of the breath became victorious over the clogged water.

Some sprinkled water and the word *mama* woke the mother.
The mother considered me a villain, whereas
bystanders called me 'Superhero.
Whatever they thought of me, I learned a life lesson.
All the breaths around, irrespective of their
differences, were united to find one breath.
If the child's breath had been taken, then mine would
have been too, as I was the lifeguard on duty.

Chapter 6

❦

You Make Me Whole

Fortified by You

"Family is the first essential cell of human society," states Pope John XXIII. At the time of our birth, our family has the responsibility of nurturing us and guiding us through every stage of life. They shower us with love and care and create a platform for us to grow and excel in life. Our family is our first school. They impart to us values, beliefs, and character and provide lessons that prepare us to face the blows of life. This selfish world sometimes can be insensitive and impetuous; our family acts as our support and our strength. As a fort shields a king and his kingdom, likewise, our families fortify us from the wickedness around.

Our families provide a safe haven where we can express ourselves freely, share our ups and downs, and receive comfort in times of despair. The bond we share with our family members helps us to feel secure and enables us to fight against the challenges of life with greater resilience. This fortification is provided to us by our families to empower us and cause us to grow and prosper. It is through the love, concern, and guidance of our family that we obtain the support to navigate the world and get past any negative vibes from our surroundings. Family also instills within us a sense of acceptance, boosts us emotionally, and shields us from worldly adversities.

An apt example is a newborn child. With his cries and gestures, he expresses his total dependence on his family. The family offers protection and comfort to the infant and continues to provide support and care until the grave. "Family is a life jacket in the stormy sea of life," J.K. Rowling writes. I would say that family is the obbligato of an individual's life. An obbligato is an essential part of a piece of music, intended for a single instrument that must not be left out. It accompanies the vocal performance. Our lives are like a vocal performance. Our families make it harmonious, so therefore the family becomes the obbligato that brings meaning to our life.

Mom and Dad, I have you as my shadow, keeping an eye on me even when I am not aware of your presence near me. My brothers and sisters, you serve as my crutches in times of trial and tribulation, as you are beside me for me to hold onto when I am about to fall. My extended family, you are my echo; whenever I call you, you call me back to comfort me.

There is an inspiring anonymous quote—"Family: where life begins and love never ends." The best exemplification of this is a mother. She brings the child to life and loves it until her last heartbeat. If her child should go astray, she will look at him with mercy and do whatever she possibly can to save him. I know of a mother who always asks that I pray for her son. Even though her son had borrowed a large amount of money from her and was not in no position to repay it, she still loved him. She had no resentment toward him.

In a family, we love and are loved. Consider this imagery to describe a family: "Families are like branches on a tree. We grow in different directions, yet our roots remain as one." Another comparison to ponder is that family members are like arteries, the blood vessels that transport oxygenated blood away from the heart and to the other parts of the body. If any artery is affected, then the supply of blood is stopped by that particular organ. As a result, the entire body feels pain. The family is like a human body. Just as if one artery is not functioning, the whole circulatory system is affected, if one member of a family is facing a problem, then the whole family is affected. If we ponder on this, it becomes evident why people say to us, "Please pray for my son [or daughter]." This is an expression of a profound bond.

Whether we are from affluence or penury, whether we are Caucasian or Asian, whether we have faith in the divine or have faith in the world, and whether we are a joint parent, a nuclear parent, or a single parent, we all have to accept the fact that we cannot change our family members, but we do have the liberty to become someone ourselves.

Applause or a Pinch

The ideal family is one that encourages and, at the same time, reprimands. Applause elevates an individual's spirit and causes him or her to want to do well in the future. A pinch reminds a person of the pain felt by his or her family on account of his or her wrong behavior. Every person deserves a chance to grow and also deserves correction to mend his or her ways. The family is the place where the individual is shaped and formed. Appreciation plays a great role in an individual's life. Encouragement is important for developing a positive outlook on oneself and increasing one's confidence in one's God-given abilities. Every gesture of support or word of recognition from family members motivates a person to pursue his or her dreams and explore his or her talents. The encouragement builds an environment where all the family members feel important and are boosted with confidence to take up future endeavors.

Constant encouragement increases an individual's effectiveness. A few words of praise lead one to be more diligent in his or her work. The work one does for one's family becomes more meaningful. Psychologists have realized that an individual's mood changes when positive words are spoken. Positive words boost a person's confidence. Negative comments kill an individual's creativity. But creativity is enhanced when a person puts his or her heart and soul into family matters.

Appreciation inculcates trust in relationships. Paul. J. Zak, a neuroscience professor at Claremont Graduate University, states: "Neuroscience shows that recognition has the largest effect on trust when it occurs immediately—after a goal has been met, when it comes from peers, and when it's tangible, unexpected, personal, and public."

Reprimands or constructive feedback are important to help a person learn from his or her mistakes. When correction is provide with love and respect, it can serve as valuable guidance, teaching the person about the consequences of his or her actions and giving him or her a chance for self-reflection. Constructive criticism enables the individual to develop accountability and a sense of responsibility in terms of his or her actions.

The one who applauds others gains by doing so. In applauding others, the focus on oneself is shifted onto others. This is a sign that one is open to allow others to grow with him or her. The mindset shifts from self-centered to other-centered. Where there is an air of positivity in the family, it enables the members to go out of their way to help others. Appreciation brings positive emotions out of a person, causing frowns to turn into smiles. The roots of all goodness lie in the soil of appreciation.

Pinching someone for his or her wrongdoings is a remedy practiced in the past. A sculptor shapes stone and causes it to look pleasing. In the same way, correction is important in the family by shaping a pleasing character. Parents correct their children out of love. When spouses correct each other, it should be done out of love and not to put each other down.

The family need not be perfect, but it does need to be united. Clarisse's husband occasionally would drink and make a lot of noise at home. If the neighbors were to ask her what happened the night before, her answer would be, "We were watching a funny movie."

She would never air her dirty laundry in front of others. And if someone was persistent in asking, her reply would be, "Why should I tell you what is cooking at our house?" This is a sign of unity among family members. Every family has its own ups and downs. It does not mean that the entire world should know.

Accepting one's mistakes and changing one's ways is a huge part of correction. Let me help you understand this with an example: The house was in silence. Tap was at his friend's place. His parents were home from work. They had no clue that Tap was absent. After having completed his homework, Tap was having the time of his life. After ten minutes, he entered his house in dirty, stinking clothes. He was drenched in sweat. His mom's eyes grew wide. He suspected that he might have committed some blunder. "Mom, what's the matter?" he asked.

She replied, "What did I tell you to do before going to play?"

"I don't remember anything."

"You have your mind only on your playing. You don't listen to what I say."

"Mom, I don't understand what you are saying. I usually remember what you say." Mom lifted up the neighbor's food container. "Oh, I forgot," Tap admitted.

"You didn't forget to eat what they gave you. Go and return their container right now."

Tap took the container with a half smile. Now he knew that his mother was not in a good mood. He was thinking about how to ask her to check his schoolwork. Gathering his courage, he said, "Mom, please, will you check the spelling and the grammar of my homework?"

The mother was surprised that he had the guts to ask for her help. She said with a stern voice, "Why do you want me to check your mistakes? You don't make any mistakes, right?"

"No, Mom, it is better to feel small before my own family and accept my mistakes than to be corrected in front of all my classmates and be humiliated for the mistakes I could have rectified. I know you love me." Mom was taken by his words. She kissed his forehead and hugged him.

Tap admitted his mistake of not returning the container. He also accepted his own weakness. With all humility, he appealed to his mom to help him. Most of us admit the mistakes we make. To accept our weaknesses and shortcomings is like biting a bullet, though. We have to remember that to feel sorry before our loved ones is better than to be embarrassed in front of unfamiliar people.

Encouragement and reprimand should go hand in hand. Through this combination, a family can create an atmosphere that promotes growth, emotional balance, and learning. It makes a person comfortable that the people around him or her love him or her unconditionally while acknowledging his or her achievements and, at the same time, making him or her realize the consequences of his or her wrongdoing.

House to Home

In order to transform the world, we must love our families first. Home is the place where love prevails. "I want home, not a house." These were the words of a woman from Mumbai, India, to one of my friends. Rain or shine, she would always be on time for the Eucharist service. Her husband worked abroad and drew a fat salary. Their only child was blessed with beauty and intelligence. The woman made the best use of her husband's income and invested in flats and shops in the city. By the time of her husband's retirement, she had earned money to supplement his salary by renting their assets. Being a rich woman, she lived a simple life. To her daughter, she was a stingy woman who would not give her whatever she wanted. All things were given to the daughter, but in due time. The woman was living in a one-bedroom flat. My friend asked her why she didn't purchase a new house or move into a bigger flat. To that, she replied that her desire was to have a home, not an enormous house.

We have to turn our houses into homes. All magnificent houses do not really make good homes. Sometimes a tiny house is the best home. A preacher at a retreat I attended said this in his talk on family. "It is beyond the shadow of a doubt that all the prominent virtues and the most relevant virtues in society come from the family unit, which fashions, strengthens, and preserves humanity." Virtue is what converts a house into a home. Love, sharing, caring, understanding, and trust are some of the prominent virtues that make a home. Being in a home means that you are a part of something very special with a bond where you are called to love and be loved for the rest of your life.

There are filthy rich families living in huge houses who fall short of love. The very prevalent human tendency is to seek somewhere else anything you don't find here. When there is no love, an individual tends to seek love from people outside the family. Such situations lead to problems such as lying and distrust.

Consider the following situations of two mothers and decide which is best:

Simran and Divya were wealthy working mothers. Both had sons who studied in the same preschool and school. Simran gave her child whatever he wanted just to stop him from nagging her and crying. Simran and her husband would have a whale of a time with their friends practically every weekend. The child would be at his grandparents' place. Divya loved her son yet did not provide him with whatever he wanted. By all means, she would see that she spent her weekends with her son.

The sons grew up and now were adults. Simran's son, though having everything, was restless, longing for the love that he did not get from his family. He dated women and would break up with them in no time. To fill the void within, he glommed onto cigarettes, which took him from the frying pan and into the fire. Divya's son did receive things from his parents, but only what was necessary. Divya explained to her son why he was not given everything he desired. He felt that he should earn, so he focused on money in order to have a better life. He worked hard to become someone in the future. There was no lack love from Divya. She would listen to him and teach him through her personal examples.

Now it is time to decide which family is the exemplary family.

It doesn't matter whether you are rich or poor, or whether you have an enormous house or not; what matters is whether your house has been made into a home or not. The core of a home is formed by love, warmth, and a sense of belonging rather than material things. A house is transformed into a home when the family members feel safe and secure, comfortable, and connected emotionally.

Home is a dwelling where one can express one's emotions freely, be one's true self, and find solace in times of tribulation. The warmth and care found within the walls of home ripple beyond the physical structure. A home stands on the relationships and bonds fashioned by the outpouring of love from the family members. It is possible to make a house into a home when the family shares laughter, makes themselves available to provide support, and is blessed with unconditional love. The life that is breathed into a house transforms it into a home, when there is active conversation at the dining table in celebration of achievements and comforting of loved ones.

The grandeur of a person's house or the size of a person's bank balance does not make up the substance of a home. Whether one lives in a congested apartment or in a magnificent house, the true measure of a genuine home is in the qualities of the individuals living there. Good qualities make a residence a heaven on earth. There is an anonymous quote that summarizes this theme: "Having somewhere to go is home. Having someone to love is family. Having both is a blessing."

Time Offering

Author Stephen Covey writes, "Most of us spend too much time on what is urgent and not enough time on what is important." We offer many things to our family members and think that our role as a mother or father is done once we do that. Sometimes the real issue is not the lack of things we receive but the lack of time we spend with our own. Time spent together develops a fruitful relationship and strengthens the bond of belongingness.

Children in particular flourish when they have devoted time with their elders. During this time, the moments of *I am heard, I am valued, and I am understood* bubble in the mind of the child. Quality time sorts out the misunderstandings and deepens the relationship. Spending time with one's spouse and siblings helps one to nurture and maintain healthy relationships. It opens a way to understand each other better and to offer support in times of challenge and also enables everyone to celebrate happy events together.

"If you are too busy to enjoy quality time with your family, then you need to reevaluate your priorities," says Dave Willis. This reminds me of a comment from a husband:

"After COVID-19, I don't listen to my wife. She goes on talking, and I simply say, 'Mm-hmm.' Then she says, 'I told you last time.' And I don't know what it is. We work online and are together twenty-four seven, so I do not pay attention to what she says." This couple had plenty of quantity time but no quality time. Quality time is the time spent playing, discussing, praying, etc.

Let's move on to the story of a father who got a better job, but as a result, his son lost his time with his dad. The father said, "Son, I got a good job. From now on, I will be able to provide you whatever you want." Initially, the son was happy. The new job filled the void in the relationship between them.

One bright spring day, in his father's absence, the son decided to play basketball. Earlier he would have spent that time with his father playing board games or cards.

One day, the son said, "Daddy, please come early. I want to play with you like before."

The father answered, "Son, today I am busy. I am not available to give you any time. It will be nice that from now on you can play with the neighborhood boys."

The boy kept silent. The days passed. The boy became very busy with the neighbors and never bothered his father to play with him. One day the father met with an accident and badly injured his leg. He was bedridden for four months. The son was very concerned about his father, and he said to him, "Let us play board games."

The father was really feeling lonely. He said, "Son! You like to play outdoors, right? So why do you want to play board games today?"

"Dad, I know it is hard to spend time alone. When you got your new job, I was longing to spend time with you. In those moments, I felt the dreadfulness of aloneness." The father realized his fault of not spending quality time with his son.

Making gestures such as enjoying meals together, playing board games, and involving yourself in others' hobbies and conversation, including any of the day's funny events, makes a significant impact on strengthening the family. The value of time spent with loved ones traveling is much higher than the value of the time individuals spend toiling to increase their bank balances. Taking care of our family is important, but in the bargain we must not neglect to be present for our family. If we do so, then we'll have many worldly possessions but no family to provide for, and all our efforts will have been in vain.

Be My Guide

Our extended family, which includes friends, relatives, neighbors, teachers, coworkers, and the other individuals in our social circle, plays an enormous role in our lives. These associations beyond our immediate family have the marvelous ability to influence us and contribute to our growth and well-being.

Relatives such as cousins, uncles, aunts, and grandparents in some families play a vital role in shaping a person's personality. By passing on their family heritage and strengthening family ties, they boost the individual, contribute to his or her personality, and infuse in all family members a feeling of belonging.

Neighbors are a part of our extended support network by voluntarily offering to help us in times of need. They cultivate a secure environment for the neighborhood. They weave the social fabric of our being, which enables us to assimilate into the broader groups of society.

Coworkers, teachers, and other professionals with whom we interact often have our professional development in mind. Teachers impart knowledge and foster our talents and make us mature people. Coworkers, in a way, provide mentorship and a sense of belonging in our professional lives.

There will be times in our lives when our family members are not close by to help us and when people from our extended networks are the ones who come to our aid. We may not know the people all over the world, but we do have a few around us whom we know and who know us. It is healthy not to compare ourselves with them but to accept them with all their strengths and weaknesses. If we don't learn to appreciate others, then we will hinder our own growth. Appreciation leads to acceptance, and this causes us to focus on our own strengths rather than on others'.

Friends are like family members we have chosen. They hold our hands and become our best companions on the unpredictable journey of life. When our tears roll down our faces and reach our cheeks, they wipe them away gently and rejuvenate our emotions. They strengthen us when required with their advice and perspective, and they cool us down when we are in a cantankerous mood. They are the wellspring of laughter and inspiration and a shoulder to cry on beyond those of our blood ties. Here I would like to present a few words about friendship from my close friend Nitesh Rodrigues:

> It is easy to make friends but difficult to maintain those friendships. Friendship is a precious gift from God to humanity. And I thank God for giving me such wonderful friends, without whom my life is incomplete. Cannio and I have been friends for

the past twenty years and are still going strong. For me, friendship is not an emotion, but a bond. We constructed our friendship on trust, respect, and love. We each know there is someone who will understand us, guide us, and be with us without judgment. Some of my relatives know my best friends without having met them. A friend is a person who stands by you when the whole world is against you, who will never misguide you, who is not sympathetic but empathetic, and whom you can rely on anytime for guidance, sharing, or just lean a shoulder to cry on. For me, friendship adds color and gives meaning to life.

We express our opinions, ideas, and thoughts without expecting the other to agree with them, and we do not impose them on each other because we know we are unique and we respect our individuality. So, we disagree, argue, and tease each other, and that is how we grow as human beings. We do not have to wear masks or please each other in order to be accepted. And of course, there is no room for jealousy. We rejoice in each other's successes; we encourage each other to do better at the same time as we correct each other; we analyze our lives; and we suggest adopting better ways to do things.

Bitter Truth

People cherish truth when it is about others. Truth becomes bitter, however, when it is about our own weaknesses. The perception and reception of truth depends on the context and the person's involvement. When one relates the truth to others, it becomes easier to accept them and not judge them. There are times when the truth blinds us so totally that we do not even question the facts of the stories we hear about others. When someone throws light on our own shortcomings, we find it to be a bitter pill to swallow and think up a thousand ways to disprove what they've said. When our failure is thrown in our faces, it can lead us to criticize ourselves and develop an inferiority complex. The bitter truth about ourselves is like a slap to our ego, which is hard to tolerate and may cause us to turn to arrogance.

Our friends or coworkers may tell the truth about us. And sometimes they tell us the truth, not to destroy us, but to build us up and make us realize that we can do better. When I was a child, I loved to get injections, but not to take syrups. Syrups are bitter and unpalatable. My mom would pinch my nostrils together to feed me the syrups. I never liked to drink them, but they were good for my health, which my mom well knew. A somewhat similar thing happens with us when we hear the truth about ourselves. We do not like to hear about our limitations, but knowing what they are helps us to become better people.

There is a way to tell the truth about others. When you correct someone with love, keeping in mind the person's future, then he or she will accept the truth well. If you correct someone with jealousy and with the thought of putting him or her down, then he or she will likely reject the truth. Respectably, the first one is a response, and the second is a reaction to a truth that the other person sees as bitter.

When I was in college, there were some among us who would insult each other by way of facial expression. There was a boy who was dark in complexion, and they called him a crow. One they called "Gas" since he farted while playing soccer. Another one was called Ladies, because he would feel shy in the presence of girls. Because of my name, I was called Khannio, which means stories in Konkani. None of these is an example of a bitter truth.

One of our professors invited the boys to join the practices for the group carol singing competition. Those who thought they could sing better than others showed up to the practices. Sam, who from a young age had been involved in the church choir, was also present for the practices. After listening to every student individually, the professor informed Sam privately that he could not be in the competition. That gave Sam the shock of his life. This was a real, bitter truth, and it was difficult to accept. Then the professor explained to Sam that singing in the church choir and singing in the competition were two different things. It was the truth with regard to Sam's weakness, and he could not bear it.

Here is another example: Two neighbors whose parents had a tradition of sharing food items with each other continued that tradition. One of them had a tendency to procrastinate. Not today, but tomorrow—then tomorrow would never come and she would not return the neighbor's cooking vessels. One of the vessels that had not yet been returned was of great sentimental value to the neighbor. This woman, upon encountering her neighbor, said, "Please be nice and return my vessel as soon as possible." It was like a slap in the face of her neighbor. With a grumpy look on her face, she returned the vessel immediately. From then onward, there was no more exchanging of food between those two families.

How one responds to the bitter truth makes all the difference. Does one take correction as an offense, or does one take it as an opportunity to improve? Because of a tiny correction, the relationship that had existed for ages between the two neighbors was ruined.

We have the tendency to make an issue of a tissue. If our tiny weaknesses go unattended, it can cause a huge amount of damage to our relationships. And sometimes the damage is irreparable.

Relief from Anguish

We all need shoulder to cry on. Each of us must face the waves of anguish that are part of life. In sharing our pain, we lighten our hearts. Life's furious fire does not burn us but makes us stronger to face future challenge. In troubled times, if someone gives us a shoulder to cry on and lends a listening ear, they give us a momentary blessing. Relief from anguish, with the help of others, lightens our hearts and creates room for empathy and understanding. This leads to the idea that we are not alone in our suffering. There are others who envelop us like a plaster of paris cast, which holds a broken limb still until it gets strong. Similarly, until we recover from our brokenness, our loved ones surround us.

Pouring our anguish into the palms of others deepens our acquaintance and benefits our relationship. Through the trust shown in sharing our emotions with others, we flatten the hills and fill the valleys of pessimistic emotions and instead foster optimistic passions. Selecting someone who is compassionate, nonjudgmental, and kind enough to listen to us is essential. It is also important to know that giving valuable advice is not everyone's cup of tea. In extreme cases, it is advised to seek help from a professional such as a therapist or counselor who provides a safe, confidential space to let go of emotion and pain.

The people who love us are always ready to lend us their ears and hear our grief-filled words. To be alone in our depression can be destructive. To have others around us is a blessing. In anguish, our minds narrow. This leads our faculties of reason to stop functioning. Other than one thought, no other thoughts are able to take over. Unless we share our internal wound with someone else, we will find it difficult to be at peace.

Following is the testimony of a girl who was on the verge of committing suicide:

> I am from one of the metropolitan cities in India.
> Growing up amid diverse cultures and religions was
> a blessing. My horizons were broad enough to allow
> me to easily accept people of other faiths. When I
> was in grade twelve, I fell for a Muslim boy. My
> parents, who are staunch Catholics, got the shock

of their lives when they found out that I had a date with this boy. To them, it was a red light in terms of any possible marriage. I insisted that I wanted to date this boy, and they tried everything they could think of to convince me otherwise. He and I eloped. Three months passed, and then came the worst time of my life. My husband ditched me for a younger woman. I was in the middle of the road and had nowhere to go. I felt orphaned. A negative thought popped into my mind. Without knowing the repercussions, I decided to give up on my life. To ease my Catholic conscience, I thought to say sorry to Jesus in the Blessed Sacrament before I took my next step.

It was around two thirty in the afternoon. The church school had just let the children out for the day. When I came out from the Blessed Sacrament, I saw children standing around pell-mell, looking for their parents. I noticed one child sharing everything that had happened at school with her mother, who was waiting for her other, older child to come out of the school.

Something within me stirred my emotions. My inner voice asked me, *Did you share with anyone what is going on inside you?* I thought that the best way to share it was in the sacrament of reconciliation. I was sure that the priest would keep my confession secret and that my story would end there when I ended my life. By then, it was three o'clock, right after lunch break, and the church office had just reopened. I called for a priest to make my confession. I confessed, and the priest said, "Though you may think that no one in this world loves you, remember that God loves you as you are." Those words ushered in the Copernican Revolution because I had been under the impression that no one loved me. In sharing, I had gained confidence and the courage to walk home to my parents and ask for forgiveness.

In sharing our sorrows, we not only lighten our hearts but also reach the threshold of emotional healing. It allows us to experience future storms of distress with greater resilience and enables us to see the future from different angles.

I AND YOU

I was placed in your arms.
You nurtured me and protected me from harm.

I cried and plunged into your bosom.
You kissed me, and then I felt awesome.

I did right, but sometimes I fought.
You tapped me and slapped me and thought.

I felt depressed and lonely.
You embarrassed me solely.

I felt it difficult to admit my mistakes.
You told me it's OK to make mistakes.

I chose you as my folks.
You adjusted to me and are my best folks.

Chapter 7

~

I Am Nothing
without You

The chapter title "I Am Nothing without You" is a profound statement expressing our total dependence and reliance on the divine power. Our existence is an intimately bonded relationship with the Almighty, from whom we receive our worth. By confessing that we are nothing without God, we admit our limitations and place the remote control to our lives in His hands.

The attitude of this statement is one of humility, considering oneself infinite and imperfect. This is in contrast to the infinite, perfect aspects of the divine. The statement also implies gratitude for the guidance and blessings of the Almighty. People with faith feel that their connection with the divine gives purpose to their lives and guides them in navigating life's challenges.

The idea of *I am nothing without You* is a reflection of the significant role of the Almighty in our lives and confirmation of our belief in God's providence.

Alpha and Omega

God reveals Himself as the Alpha and the Omega. Alpha is the first letter of the Greek alphabet, and Omega is the last. God is the beginning and the end. He is beyond time and space. God is the foundation of all existence, circumscribing all things from the beginning to the end. This means that God is not bound by anything in the universe, but is above it. All creatures are subject to His magnificent power.

When we say that God is the beginning, it means He was present before everything. To state that He is the end means that without Him, nothing exists and everything comes to an end.

The Alpha and the Omega characteristics of God facilitate His omnipotence, omnipresence, and omniscience, that is, total power, constant presence, and total knowledge of everything.

Revelation 21:6–8 reads, "It is done. I am the Alpha and the Omega, the Beginning and the End. To the thirsty I will give water without cost from the spring of the water of life. Those who are victorious will inherit all this, and I will be their God and they will be my children. But the cowardly, the unbelieving, the vile, the murderers, the sexually immoral, those who practice magic arts, the idolaters and all liars—they will be consigned to the fiery lake of burning sulfur. This is the second death." This verse describes the omnipotent quality of God. He knows His flock, and He knows who has gone astray. He knows everything because all exists under His sight. He perceives all things, both visible and invisible, and knows all things in minute detail. God possesses comprehensive knowledge that surpasses the human intellectual capacity.

The omniscient quality of God comforts believers, as it implies that God knows our needs and our circumstances. He is also aware of our deepest thoughts, our struggles, and our dreams. This belief may differ from religion to religion, but the concept of God's all-knowing nature is a common aspect.

Revelation 1:8 reads, "I am the Alpha and the Omega, says the Lord God, who is and who was and who is to come, the Almighty." This passage explains the omnipresent quality of God. The declaration "who is" indicates that God is constantly present in the present moment. Not confined to time, He is here and now, dynamically involved in the events that are occurring. The statement "who was" indicates that God was there in the past, hovering over everything throughout history. Not restricted to time, He transcends it and is aware of what occurred in the past. The phrase "who is to come" signifies that God is already in the future. He knows what is in store for the future. This points out that God cannot be surprised by the future; He has a plan for what will happen in the future.

Revelation 22:11–13 reads, "Let the one who does wrong continue to do wrong; let the vile person continue to be vile; let the one who does right continue to do right; and let the holy person continue to be holy. Look, I am coming soon! My reward is with me, and I will give to each person according to what they have done. I am the Alpha and the Omega, the First and the Last, the Beginning and the End." These verses express God's attribute of omnipotence. God has power over everything, even the fallen angles. He projects boundless power and authority over all things, living and nonliving, that make up the universe, including metaphysical powers. There is no boundary to God's power, and there is nothing outside His control. God retains definitive power over all physical and spiritual beings. This power He patents, such as judgment, redemption, and execution of His plan.

You Exist

Our existence is completely reliant on God. Someone said it rightly: "I am alive just because God is merciful toward me." God's existence cannot be comprehended by the human brain. Only in faith can we perceive metaphysical realities. No one can satisfactorily prove or disprove the existence of God. The very fact that we say "God is this" and "God is that" shows that we make the mistake of compartmentalizing God, who is more than we can imagine. God is indefinite and can only be experienced. When we say that no one can prove God's existence, it does not mean that we deny the five arguments in favor of God's existence posed by Thomas Aquinas in *Summa Theologica*. These arguments are the argument of motion, the argument of causation, the argument of contingency vs. necessity, the argument of perfection, and the argument of design. We also do not disapprove of the ontological argument of Saint Anselm of Canterbury. In his claim that God exists, he says that God is "a being than which no greater can be conceived and which exists." These arguments are made in light of the philosophical realm. They give us a glimpse of the reality but not the entire truth of God's existence.

It is like a man stepping into a river and realizing that the water is up to his knees. This does not mean that when the river merges with the ocean, the water will be at the same level. Here, water is the common factor. The man knows the depth of the river water, which is undeniable, but is not aware of the depth of the same water in the ocean. Likewise, we cannot deny the foregoing arguments because through these arguments we come to know something of God. But this means the arguments don't provide us with a total knowledge of God. The arguments provide partial knowledge but not the entire truth.

Faith plays a vital role in our grasping of metaphysical realities, even the existence of God. Faith includes accommodating truths based on religious doctrine, belief, and spiritual encounters.

Christian mysticism has a different story to tell about God's existence. Intellectuals consider Pseudo-Dionysius to have been a Syrian monk. During the late fifth century, he wrote on mystical theology. He took his name from Saint Dionysius the Areopagite. In his writings, he talks about the divine name causing problems with regard to religious knowledge and language by way of divergent divine transcendence. In itself, God's nature is incomprehensible, but He manifests in all existing beings as their cause. In other words, God is transcendent and present in all things at the same time. It is the paradox in which Dionysius's affirmative and negative theology is hidden. Affirmative theology centers on divine causality and speculates that God exists through divine manifestation. Affirmative theology establishes various names for the divine such as "love" and "good." In his work *Mystic Theology*, he negates all names for God, saying that divinity, because it is transcendent, cannot be understood. According to Dionysius, God is nameless, as well as praised in all names. The inaccessibility of God by way of human thought and the importance of approaching Him remains as the focal point of mystical theology.

A book by an unknown author assumed to be a fourteenth-century priest is called *The Cloud of Unknowing*. The cloud being described cannot be penetrated by intellect but by love alone. The two central themes in *The Cloud of Unknowing* are divine transcendence and the inaccessibility of God by way of human thought. We derive knowledge of God not through the cataphatic (positive ideas) or through the apophatic (negative way of emptying the self). Those who wish to know God have to abandon their intellects and approach Him through their hearts. This is done by casting every thought that comes to mind into the cloud of forgetting. Cognition has no hope of penetrating the impermeable cloud of darkness isolating us from our Creator. Love for God alone can break through the cloud of unknowing, and at last, God reaches out to us from the other side.

The author writes in the fourth chapter,

> And our soul by virtue of this reforming grace is
> made sufficient to the full to comprehend all of Him
> by love, which is incomprehensible to all created
> knowledgeable powers, as an angel, or man's soul;
> I mean, by their knowing, and not by their loving.
> And therefore I call them in this case knowledgeable

powers. But yet all reasonable creatures, angel and man, have in them each one by himself, one principal working power, which is called a knowledgeable power, and another principal working power, which is called a loving power. Of the two powers, to the first, which is a knowledgeable power, God that is the maker of them is evermore incomprehensible; and to the second, the which is the loving power, in each one diversely He is all comprehensible to the full. In so much that a loving soul alone in itself, by virtue of love, should comprehend in itself Him that is sufficient to the full—and much more, without comparison—to fill all the souls and angels that ever may be.

The Cloud of Unknowing encourages to live a contemplative life and seek holiness at an existential level, then physical knowledge, which is far from words and images.

Many religious beliefs acknowledge that a total conception of God's existence is beyond human reach. Therefore, God is considered the foundation of our existence, the One who brings us to life and sustains our being.

Hindu mysticism expresses similar thoughts. According to Advaita Vedanta, only God is *sat* (Sanskrit for real, true, and right). Everything else is *asat,* such as the mind, the body, and all the various living things. This means that only God is real. All other existing things lean on God for their existence. That's how the things other than God become unreal. Without God's continuous presence, our existence is null and void. Though we can have partial knowledge of God, our existence is entirely dependent on Him. The different religions may have subtle differences in terms of perspective on the human being's dependence on God's providence. However, in general, most of the religions believe in human beings' dependence on a higher power. It is like a swimming pool with God as the cap.

If the cap is taken off, then the pool becomes empty. Without the cap, water can't exist in the pool, so by extension, without Him we can't exist.

Only You

When I am lonely, You are the only one with whom I can talk. My loved ones cannot be everywhere I go, but You are there everywhere I go. When things are beyond my reach, then only You can save me. This type of talking with God takes place in the form of prayer.

Prayer is considered by many religions to be the primary way to communicate with God. It is understood as the way of expressing one's thoughts, desires, emotions, and apprehensions to the Almighty. Time spent in prayer allows an individual to reflect on his or her life, get guidance, and gain enlightenment as to the present circumstances. It is a way to seek inner peace and the resilience to face one's challenges, and to enjoy some company in times of loneliness. In times of loneliness, belief in God's presence acts as a comfortable cushion. Most religions teach that God is present at every moment of our lives and is attentive to our prayers, particularly when our loved ones cannot be present with us.

Saint Teresa of Avila talks about contemplative prayer: "Mental prayer, in my opinion, is nothing else than an intimate sharing between friends; it means taking time frequently to be alone with Him whom we know loves us. The important thing is not to think much but to love much and therefore do that which best stirs you to love. Love is not a great delight but a desire to please God in everything." We have to share our ups and downs as well as our achievements with the One who loves us.

"Then I joined my hands and prayed." These are the words of one of my parishioners who migrated to foreign country at the age of twenty-three in the early 1980s. Loneliness enveloped him. He felt frustrated and thought of going back to his native land. Though the church he attended was run by religious priests, he had not visited their monastery. On one occasion, he decided to pour his heart out to a priest. He stood outside the monastery and was of two minds, trying to decide whether to enter or not. The priest who had been gardening called him inside. As he entered, he ended up sharing his story, at which point he was in tears. The priest asked him to follow, and soon they reached a calm and cozy chapel. The priest held up his hands and said, "One hand is you, and the other is God. Join them and your dreams will come true. When you join your hands in prayer, you are not alone. God is with you." That was the turning point in my parishioner's life. After that, he had peace of mind.

I believe that prayer is the foundation of our being and that it has to be instilled right from the beginning. Doing this will help a child cope up with loneliness. When I was a kid, on one occasion my daddy had not returned from work. The man who was always home by eight o'clock at night showed no sign of returning until ten thirty. In those days, there were no mobile phones and our area's bus service stopped at ten at night.

I noticed my mother's hands were joined together. With her eyes wide open, she was gazing at the altar. Since it was a holiday, I had not yet hit the sack and was playing with a ball made from old socks. As I was catching the ball, I stumbled upon the cane that was used to discipline me and my siblings. My mother turned and said, "I don't want any noise here! Please come and pray that your daddy comes soon."

With a lethargic attitude, I said, "Why should I pray? Anyway, you continue your prayers." My mother did not reprimand me. Instead, she called me closer, putting her hand on my shoulder.

She said, "Jesus loved children and called them to him. He listens to children's prayers."

Without uttering a word, I knelt and prayed. In the next five minutes, my daddy was at the doorpost. If we understand the worth of prayer as children, then as adults we will know what to do when we are in turmoil.

Prayer Has No Set Place and No Set Time

Community prayer has a set time. Each person coming at their own time does not make for community prayer. In this section, the focus is on individual prayer and not community prayer.

Once a young neophyte philosopher approached a guru and asked, "What time is the best time to pray?"

The guru replied, "The time before you die."

Displeased with the answer, the philosopher responded, "But I don't know when I will die."

After taking a deep breath, the guru said, "Yes, we do not know the exact time of our death, so there is no particular time for prayer."

I would like to share something inspirational that I learned from one of my friends: that one should pray at any time and in any place. The year my friend joined the Carmelites, I also joined. He came from a close-knit family and loved to have people around him. Initially, I thought it must have been difficult for him to be living a secluded life. I was flabbergasted by a simple gesture of his. He always wore a rosary ring that had a cross on top. Whenever he remembered God, he would kiss that cross, sometimes more than six times a day. His intention for doing this was to communicate with God. Whenever he felt happy or sad, he would kiss the ring. Although the rest of us thought it was amusing, it taught us the lesson that one can pray at any time.

Years passed in the seminary. My friend and I were sent to Mumbai to study theology at Saint Pius X College. The journey from our residence to the college was difficult but quick since it was by rail, and tens of thousands of travelers made it to their destinations every day using this mode of transportation. Mumbai is known for its crowed trains. Who would think of praying on a train when there are numerous bodies all around you, bumping up against yours? And sometimes a person's breath or armpit odor makes you feel like running off the train.

Once on the boisterous, chaotic train, my friend would place his backpack on his chest and close his eyes. He would stand there praying. Though he believed that the chapel was a great place to pray as part of the community, he was convinced that there is no fixed place for private prayer. This is the humble attitude of an individual who seeks to find God in any environment.

This type of spirituality was practiced by Brother Lawrence, a seventeenth-century French Carmelite monk. With regard to his having been assigned to do the kitchen chores of cooking and cleaning, he wrote the following lines of verse:

> O Lord of pots and pans and things,
> since I have no time to be
> a great saint by doing lovely things,
> or watching late with Thee,
> or dreaming in the dawn light,
> or storming heaven's gates,
> Make me a saint by getting meals
> and washing up the plates.

In this poem, Brother Lawrence talks about finding God in pots and pans. He acknowledges his constraint of working in the kitchen and asks God into his workplace. His utmost desire was to be a saint.

Look Up in Hope

Our lives become more worthy of living and more meaningful when we have hope. The relationship that we build with the Almighty has no end. It gives us the hope that our life here on earth is just a comma and not a full stop. Our relationship with the divine brings an immense sense of hope that ignores the importance of our temporal existence on earth. The hope in life after death provides consolation and boosts the possibility of life continuing. It confirms the idea that every life has a purpose and elevates us above the suffering and limitations of the earthly realm. Hope motivates the faithful to live our lives with meaning, being aware of our actions and choices, which have enormous implications on our perspective of eternal life.

A relationship cultivated with God in prayer enables the faithful to have enduring faith. Such a bond with God offers hope for one's spiritual life in the form of redemption and the fulfillment of God's promises. Hope instills an optimistic attitude and an unwavering belief that, at last, there is an ultimate destination beyond our earthly life.

Jesus speaks of this in Luke 10:38–42. This is the episode when Jesus meets Martha and Mary at their place. As any normal woman would do upon a guest's arrival, Martha was engrossed in preparations. She felt it was too much. To lighten her burden, she requested Jesus to send her sister to assist her, as she was sitting at the feet of the Lord. Jesus replied to her, "Martha, Martha, you are worried and upset about many things, but few things are needed— or indeed only one. Mary has chosen what is better, and it will not be taken away from her." Mary loved to spend time with Jesus, so she chose to be with him. Jesus took it to another level. He told Martha that Mary chose a better option and that no one could take it away from her.

No one can take away our prayer lives. The time we spend communicating with God will never be in vain. This prayer life is also continued in heaven. Following are some passages of scripture discussing continuous prayer in heaven:

Isaiah 6:2–3 reads, "Above him were seraphim, each with six wings: With two wings they covered their faces, with two they covered their feet, and with two they were flying. And they were calling to one another: 'Holy, holy, holy is the Lord Almighty; the whole earth is full of his glory.'"

Revelation 7:11–12 states, "All the angels were standing around the throne and around the elders and the four living creatures. They fell down on their faces before the throne and worshipped God, saying, 'Amen! Praise and glory and wisdom and thanks and honor and power and strength be to our God forever and ever. Amen!'"

Let's move on to the example of a woman who remained composed even when ill. She saw suffering not as a curse but accepted it as a blessing and offered it for the salvation of others. I used to visit a mission station every month and celebrate Mass for the faithful. I would take Holy Communion to the homebound on every visit. Once I encountered an elderly woman who had been in bed for years. Her daughter would go to see her every evening. Once in a blue moon, she would be visited in the summer by a deer, which would give her pleasure whenever she saw it through the window. Though she was born in 1940s, she had updated herself, using her iPad to read the news. Her family members coached her on how to use the internet.

When I visited this elderly woman at her home, I noticed the look of serenity on her face. She had no regrets about not being a part of the high-tech world. She said, "The first thing I watch is the news. I hear of a lot of evil things happening in the world. I thank God for keeping me safe from that evil. I am grateful to God for keeping me far from temptation and making me available to pray for the people who have gone astray." Her outlook on life was absolutely astonishing. Who of us would thank God for paralyzing us? She was not only homebound but also confined to bed. I have never experienced such a graceful face in my life. I felt that she already had one foot in heaven. God instills hope in us, and our deaths become meaningful.

Faith in God brings meaning to our deaths. This perspective arises from a belief in God's existence beyond time and space. Hope comforts us, and reassurance urges us that death leads to a transition to a different state of life and is not the end.

Several religions espouse the idea that God is present during our last moments of life, offering support. This belief eliminates the horror of uncertainty that revolves around death and enables the faithful to embrace death with faith and hope. This pumps the individual full of consolation and peace as he or she makes the big adieu.

Death Never Dies

Death never dies for those who believe in life after death. Religions play a significant role in infusing hope into an individual. To the faithful who believe in eternal life, death is perceived as the threshold to a different form or state of being. Death is seen as an inevitable plunge into the afterlife, where one's soul exists in spiritual form. The choices the individual makes in life matter. Many of us are convinced that good choices lead us to heaven and that bad choices push us toward hell. Therefore, this implies that before death, we should be involved in good works.

However, the concept of life after death is subtly different in various religions, with the concept being that life continues in a different form after death. Concepts such as heaven, hell, reincarnation, purgatory, and the spiritual realm fall under the framework of different religions. Additionally, religions are keen on providing instruction for moral and ethical conduct that encourages the faithful to live meaningful lives. Religious rituals and teachings play a vital role in helping people overcome grief and loss. They provide spiritual direction and encourage faith in a higher power, which showers with comfort and healing the people who are grieving after having lost a loved one. With the help of various religious worldviews, I will try to explain the concept of life after death.

In the Abrahamic religions, Judaism, Christianity, and Islam, the faithful expect life to continue after death. The Eastern religions such as Buddhism and Hinduism believe in life after death, but it is form of reincarnation. Here death is accepted as inevitable and not as terrible. Some of the minor religions do not believe in life after death, like Confucianism and Taoism.

Confucianism is neutral about the afterlife or any sort of celestial abode where souls go after the people die. Confucianists believe in a philosophical and ethical system that stresses social order and the need for education and moral values. According to the Confucians, if an individual abides by the golden rule given by Confucius, then he or she should not be concerned about what comes next since he or she lived a righteous life amid society.

Taoism is built on a philosophical and religious tradition that accentuates living in peace with nature and the universe. Whereas some Taoists partially believe in some form of afterlife and most of them perceive death as a normal part of the cycle of life, they do not believe in a perpetual afterlife.

Buddhism believes the individual either is reincarnated or enters into a state of enlightenment, that is, nirvana. Buddhists believe in a cycle of death and rebirth, which ends only when the person achieves the ultimate goal, nirvana. In Buddhism, there is no concept of God or soul. Buddhists believe that the consciousness continues in the reincarnation cycle and also that it experiences suffering. And the goal is to flee from the cycle by reaching nirvana.

Hinduism and Buddhism have many concepts in common. The major difference is that Hindus believe in the soul and God whereas Buddhism does not. In Hinduism, they believe in reincarnation after death. The soul (atman) is embodied in a new body according to the karma the person accumulated in his or her previous life. This reincarnation can take place in any type of living being, not only human beings.

According to Hinduism, the purpose of life is to release the soul from the reincarnation cycle and attain moksha, that is, liberty from the cycle. The ultimate resting place for the soul is Brahman.

In Judaism, the existence of an afterlife depends on an individual's beliefs. However, most Jewish people believe in life after death. They believe in hell (Gehenna), a place of suffering and pain, and believe that only the righteous can enter heaven (*olam ha-ba*), "the Garden of Eden."

Both Shia and Sunni Muslims believe in an afterlife. For them, death is the end of corporeal life on earth, but the soul exists eternally. The souls go to angel of death and wait for Judgment Day. On that day, the individual's actions over the course of his or her lifetime will be judged. Muslims believe that when an individual does good while living, he or she will go to Jannah, which is paradise. If an individual is involved in wrongdoing, then his or her soul will go to Jahannam, a place of pain and suffering.

Christianity is the religion of hope. Christians believe in eternal life. One who does good deeds on earth is rewarded with heaven. And one who is engaged in evil acts is condemned to hell. Catholics believe in purgatory, a place of purification of the soul from sin.

Christianly has a distinctly different understanding of God than other religions.

Matthew 1:23 reads, "The virgin will conceive and give birth to a son, and they will call him Immanuel (which means 'God with us')." John 1:14 reads, "The Word became flesh and made his dwelling among us. We have seen his glory, the glory of the one and only Son, who came from the Father, full of grace and truth."

Imagine you were kidnapped and put in prison. For two days, you survive only on water. In that situation, the only thought revolving in your mind is how to get out. Around dawn, you have three guests come visit. One offers you the key to an exotic house; the next one offers you the key to a BMW car; and the last one offers you the key to your prison cell. Which key will you accept? Most of us would say the key to the prison cell. Yes, that is what would set us free. If we possess the key to a house or car, it would be useless if we were left to die in the prison. Jesus, though God, became like one of us and gave us the keys to our redemption. He does not promise a prosperous life here on earth by offering us the key to worldly riches; he offers life in full. John 10:10 reads, "The thief comes only to steal and kill and destroy; I have come that they may have life, and have it to the full."

Consider this example of an individual who dedicated his life to the Lord. Beyond a shadow of a doubt, he was convinced that Jesus was the true and only Redeemer. A devout Carmelite priest who was born in a high-caste family, he had a great desire to become a priest at a very young age. Though from an affluent family, he never demanded any comforts in his priestly life. He lived a simple, austere life. In his old age, he was transferred to a monastery. The first misfortune he experienced in his old age was the loss of his eyesight. He had to learn to walk again from scratch, by counting his steps and feeling his surroundings. He did not want to bother anyone, so he first learned to walk to the washroom. This person who used to spend much of his time writing was now unable to read. He used to be the first person to show up to pray in the chapel, and now he was the last. In spite of this, a blanket of calmness covered his face. He would say the words of Saint Teresa of Avila: "Let nothing disturb you; let nothing frighten you; all things are passing away: God never changes. Patience obtains all things. Whoever has God lacks nothing. God alone suffices."

Two years later, another tsunami wave came upon him. This time it was lethal. Prostate cancer had crept into his body. His situation had now gone from bad to worse. It was not only mental pain but also physical pain that he was now dealing with.

The omnipresent smile on his face said it all. He never uttered a word of discomfort. According to him, suffering was a blessing. His only reply was, "Jezu Marie, mhaka pav," which means "Jesus and Mary, come to my aid." He had a blessed vision of heaven, and that kept his spark of hope alive. He had strong faith in Jesus that he would turn his death into life eternal. God is the only You that all faithful desire to embrace after death.

YOU

You exist, and I believe
You exist. Many believe, but not as I believe.
You exist. Some disbelieve, yet we believe.
You are the beginning of beginnings and the end of ends.
You cannot be capsulated. If so, then it would not be You.
You are not this or that. You are a mystery to comprehend.
You are there when I am alone and lost.
You are the hope of a life not yet seen.
You are there at death, and death turns into eternal life.

Conclusion

"All I have is you" emphasizes the symbiotic relationship between individuals. It proposes that the self (I) is deeply rooted in others (you), highlighting the dependence and interconnectedness that define human relationships.

The concept "womb to the tomb" accentuates the lifelong nature of this interdependence. From birth to death, individuals rely on each other for support, growth, and fulfillment. This dynamic does not provide liberty to individuals to measure their worth against others that can lead to the inferiority complex.

Clapping on others' triumph and shaking hand with others on our achievements will keep us humble and others consoled. This gracious approach not only captures the hearts of others, but also leaves a lasting and positive impression.

This text endorses a viewpoint that emphasizes the significance of relationships and associations as an integral mechanism of a rewarding and purposeful life journey. It advocates that we enhance our existence, composed of both body and soul, by recognizing the importance of the Divine. The Divine holds the key to the heavenly destination, where the soul finds repose upon the body's demise.

Printed in the United States
by Baker & Taylor Publisher Services